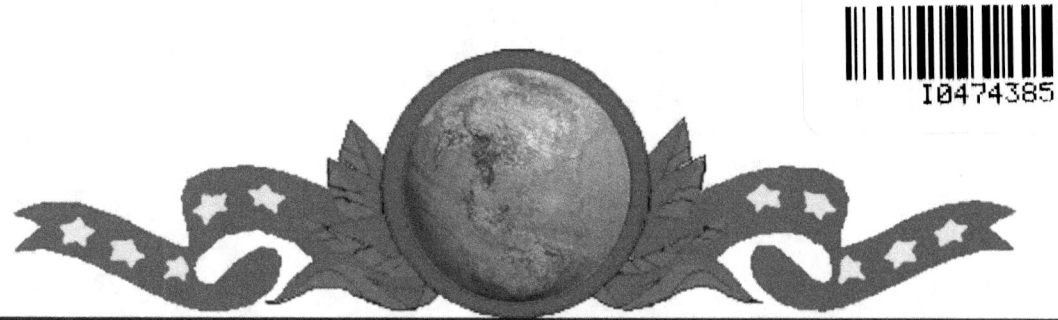

# Real World

## Colouring Book

### For Advanced Users & Adults

Copyright 2019 By John Boom

## 50 Images

## Created From Real Life Photos
## For You To Colour As You Please.

ISBN 978-0-359-97214-2

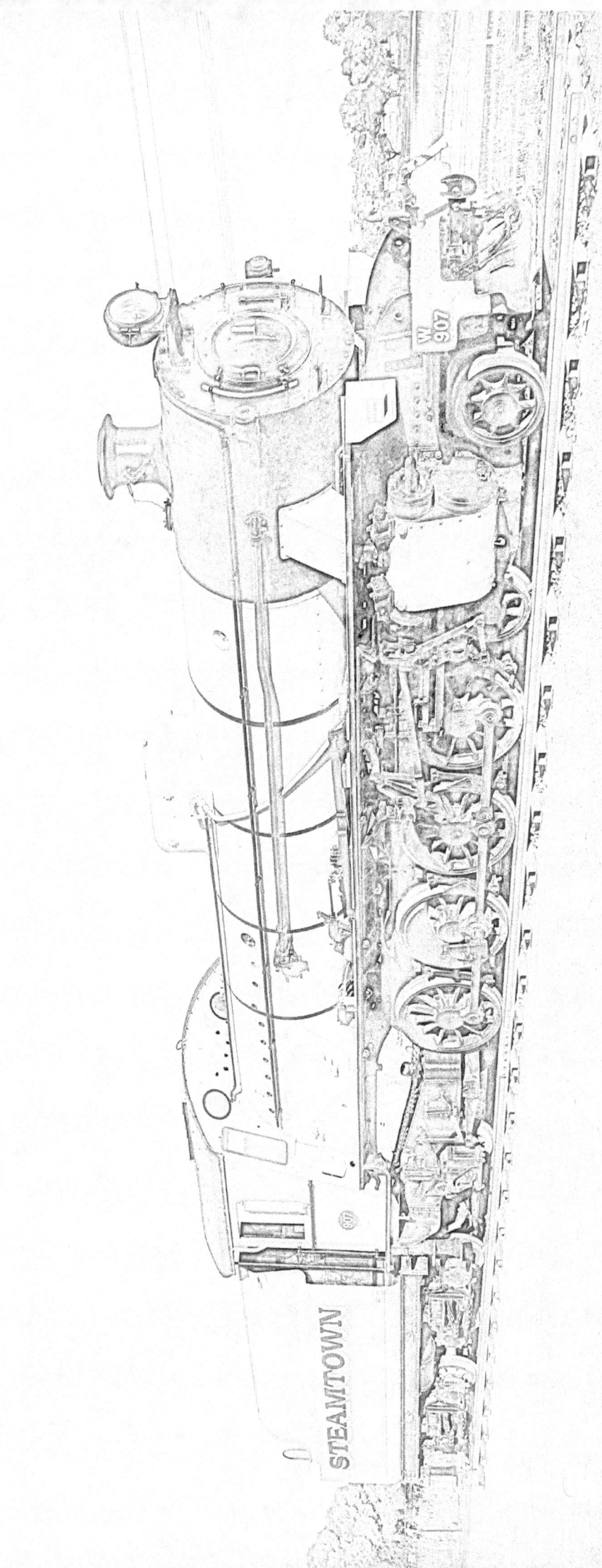

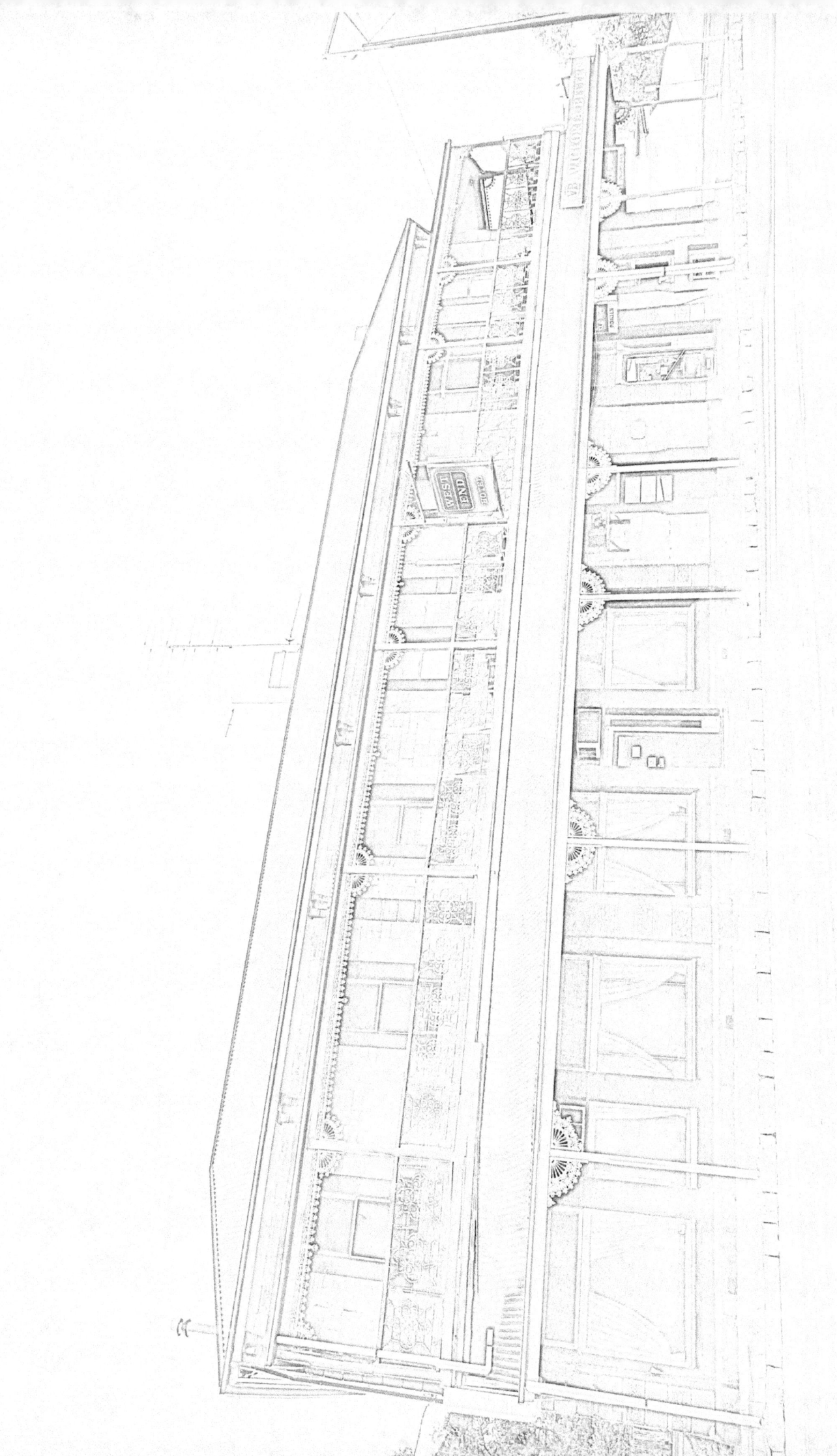

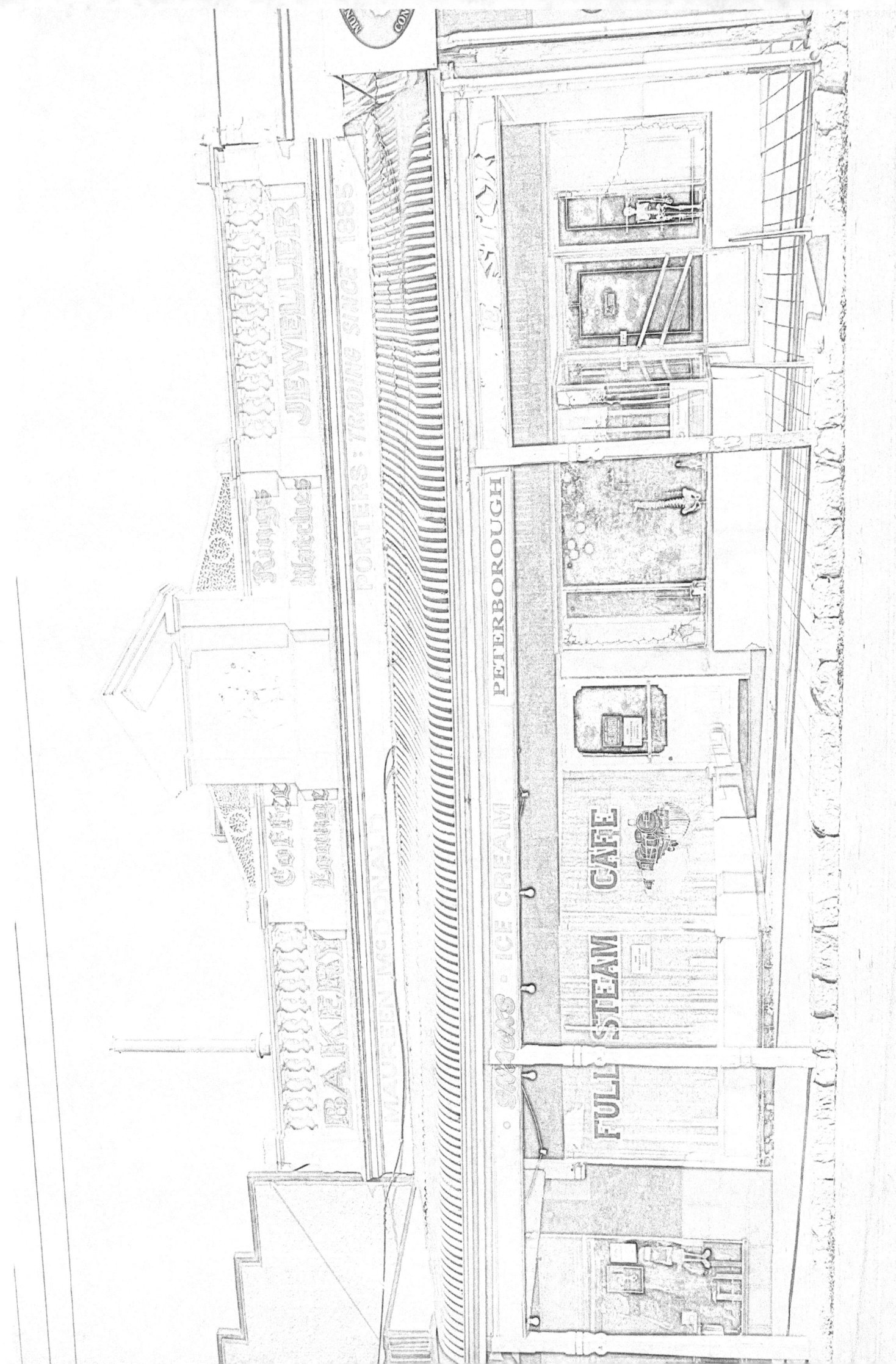

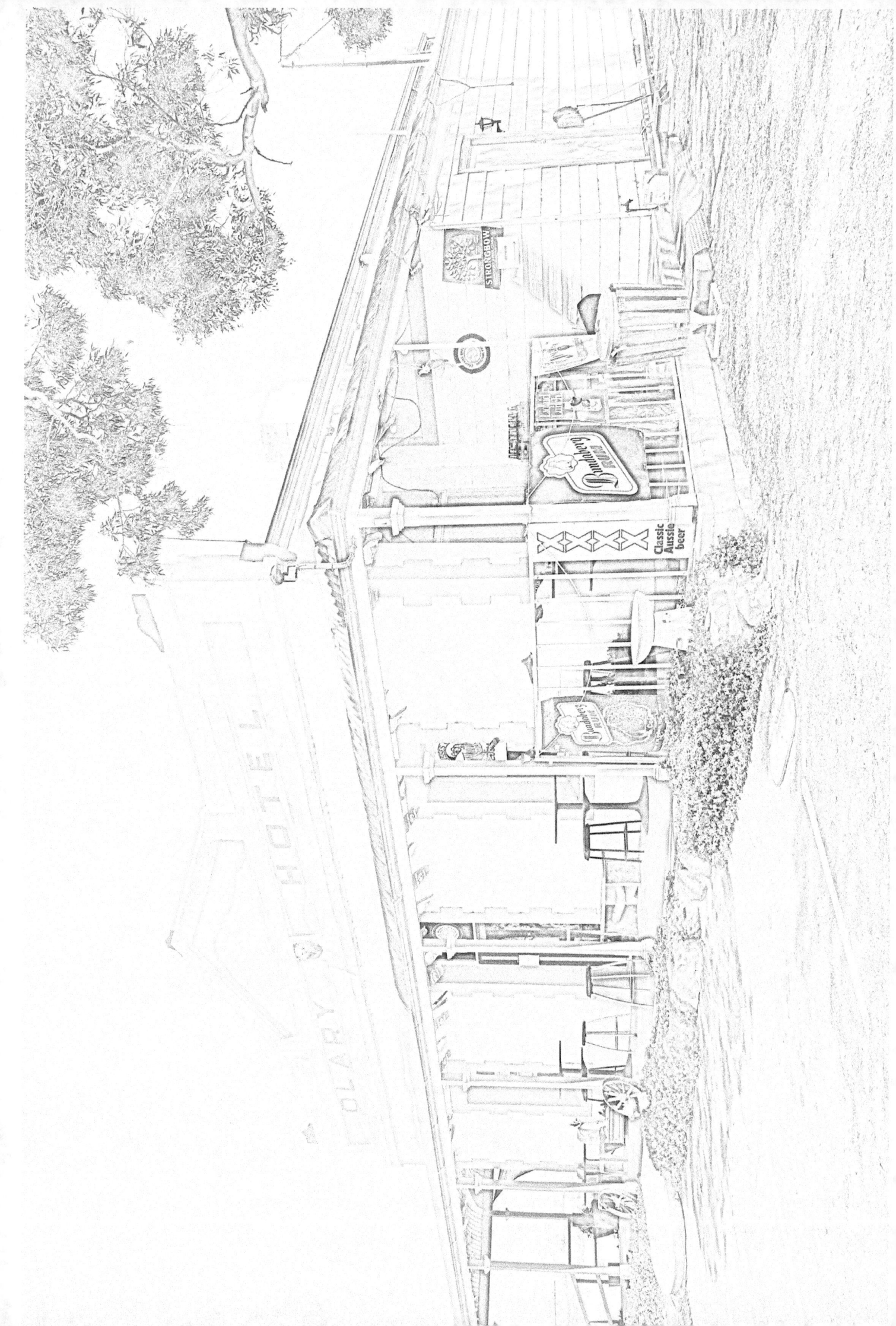

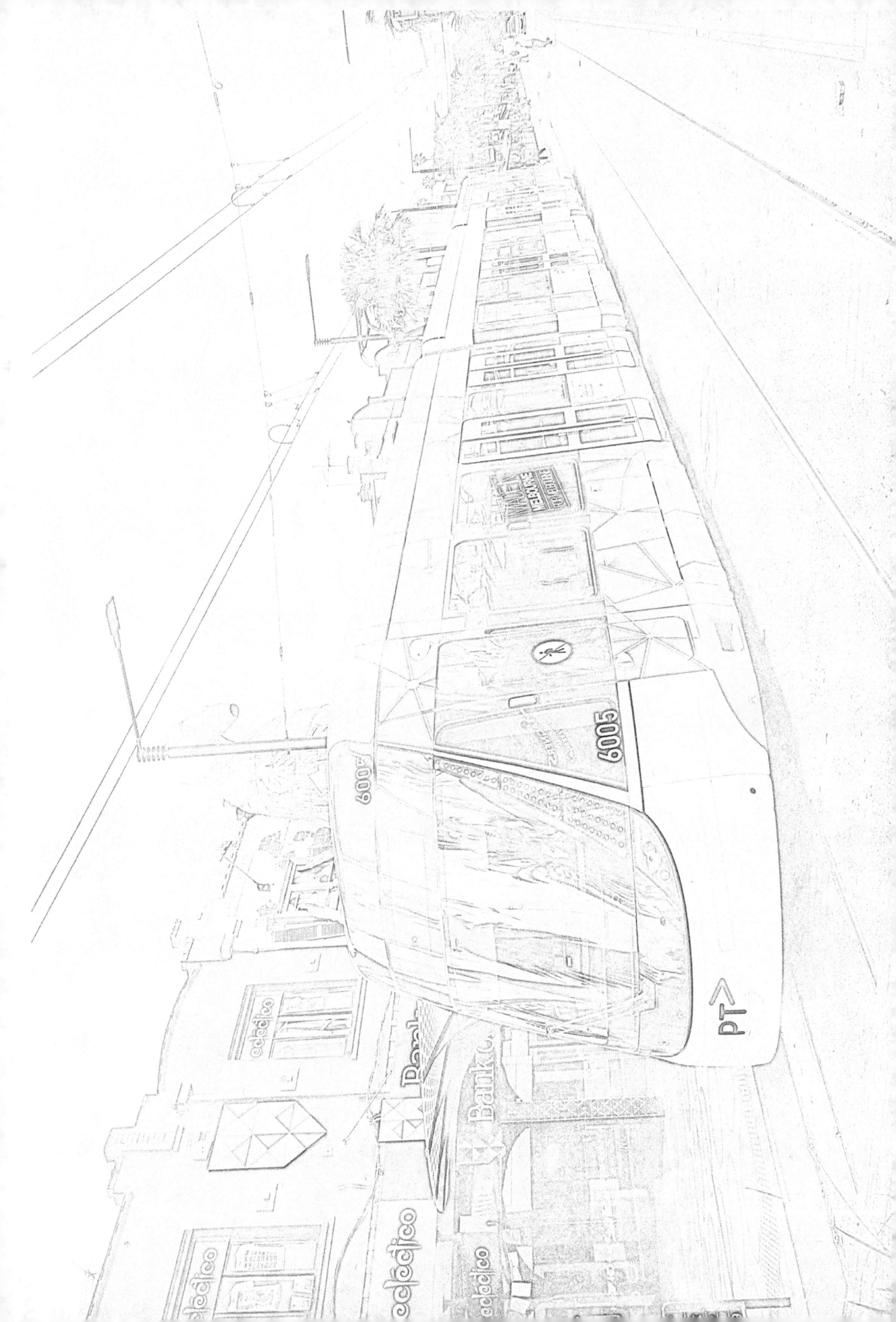

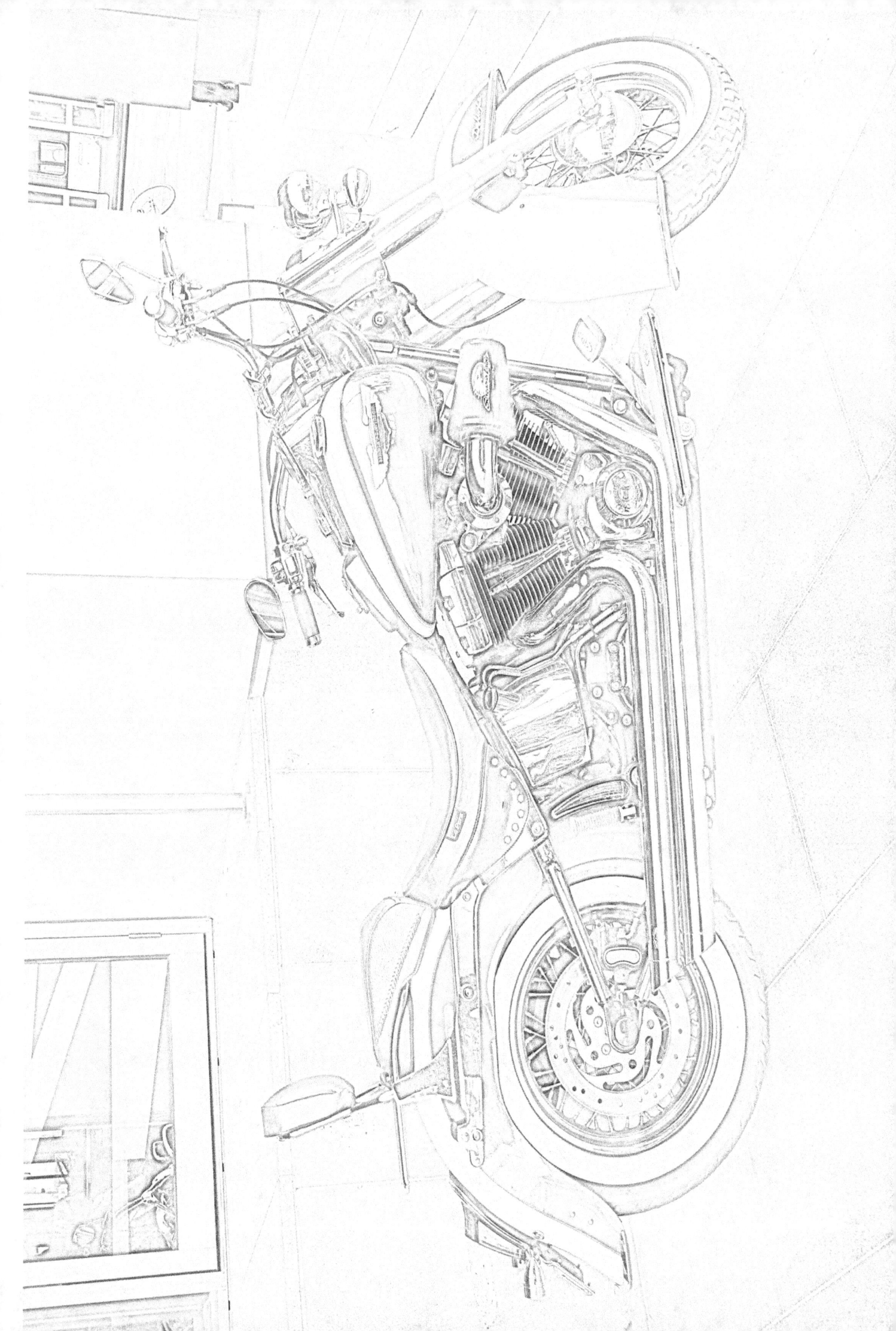

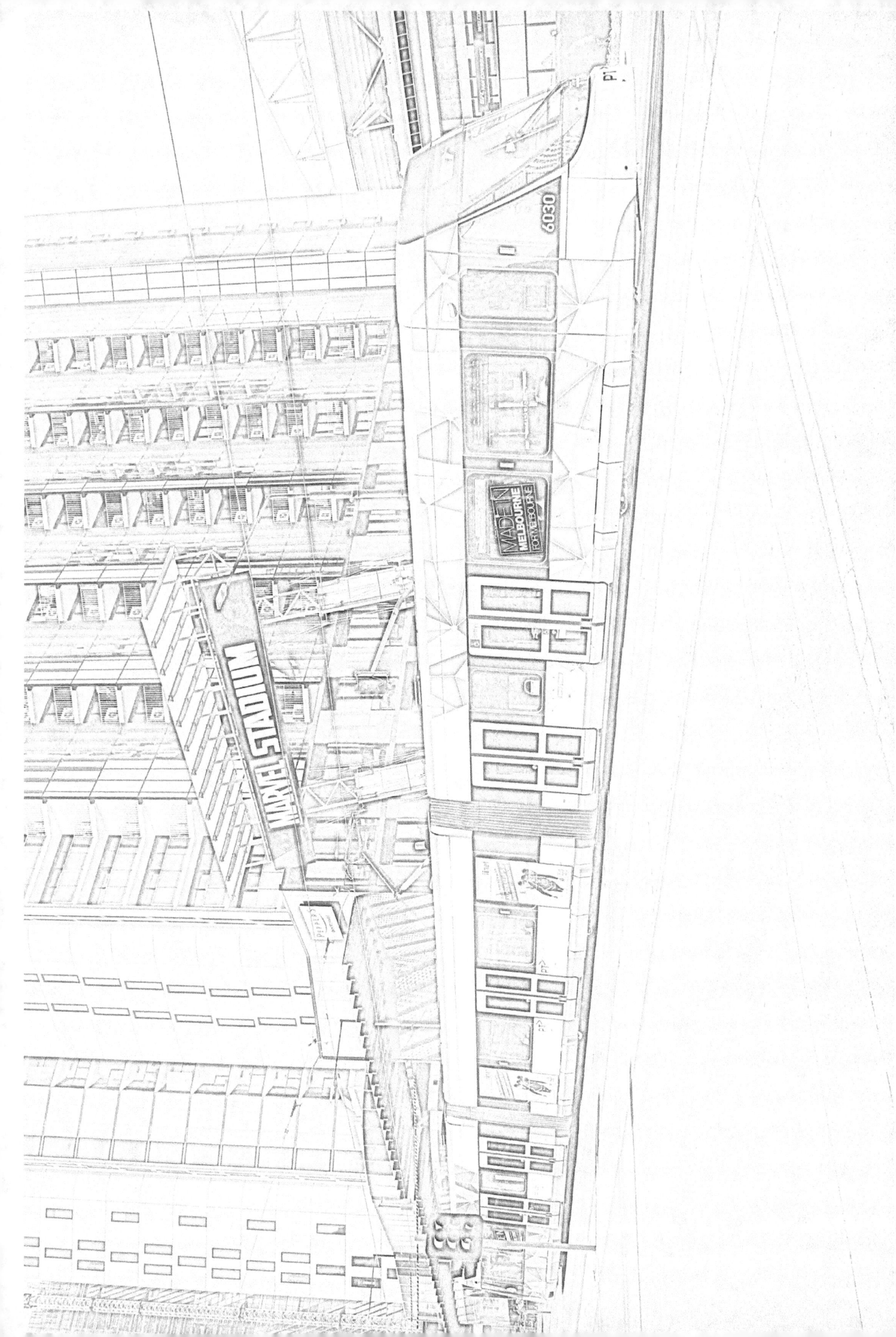

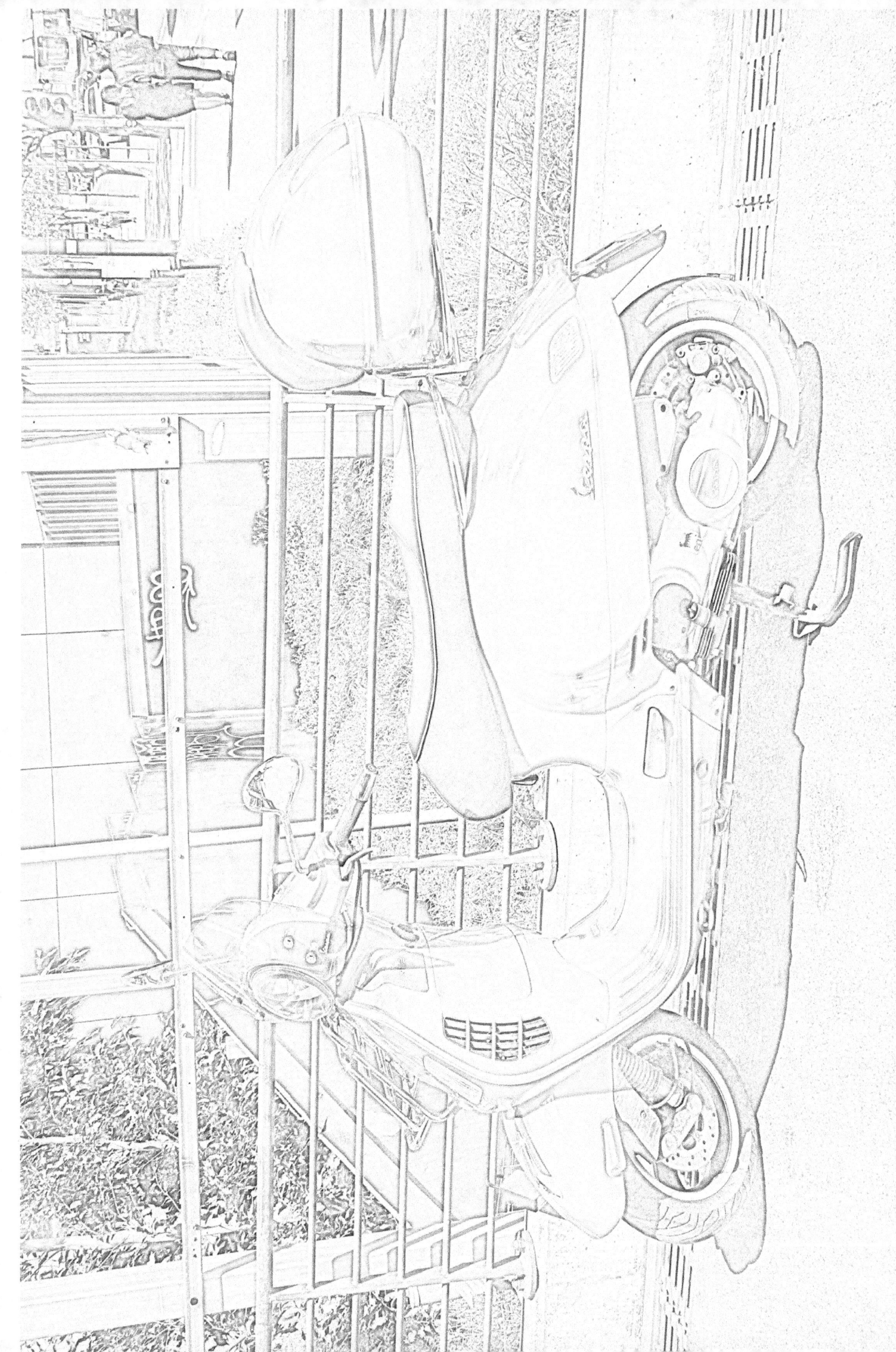

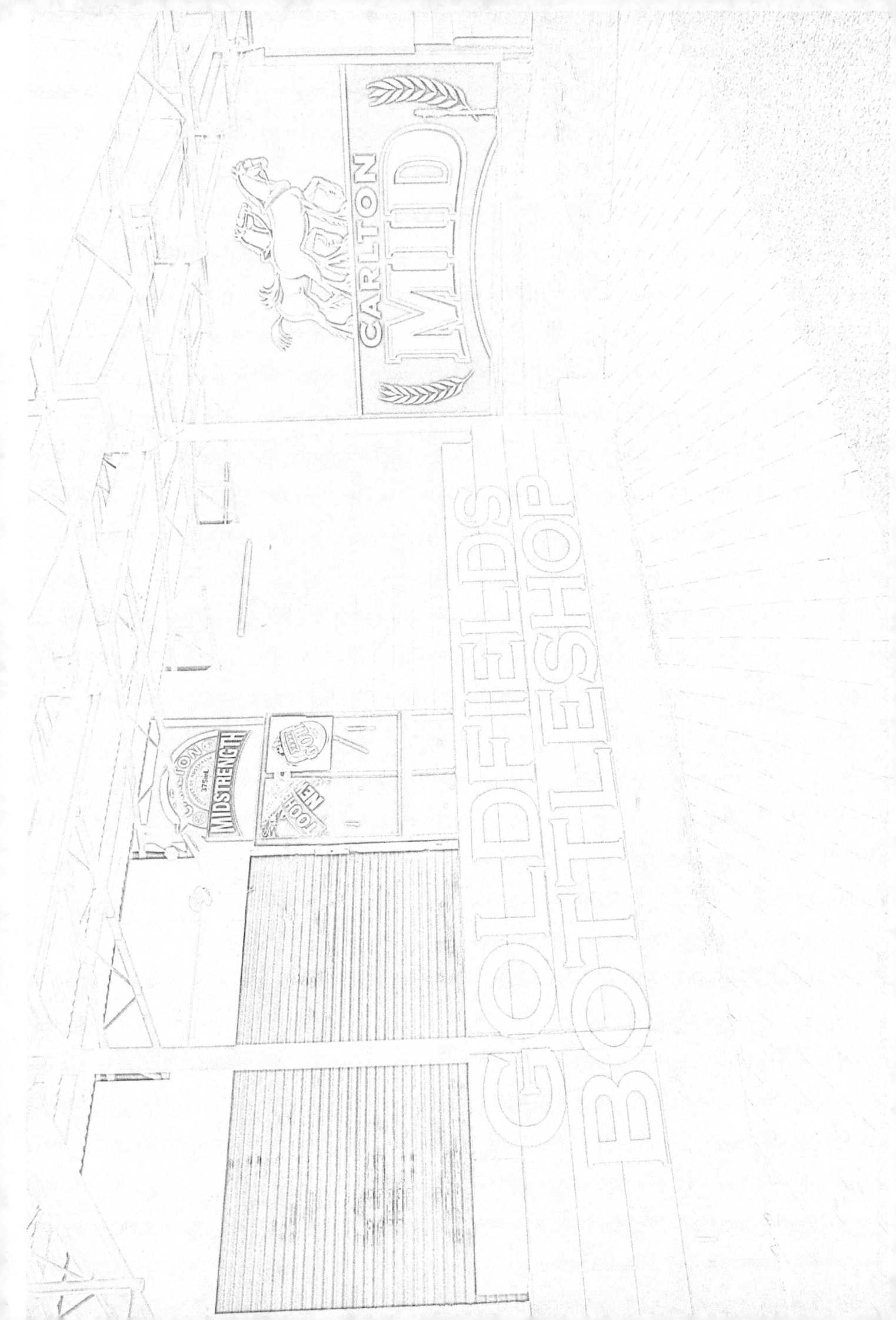

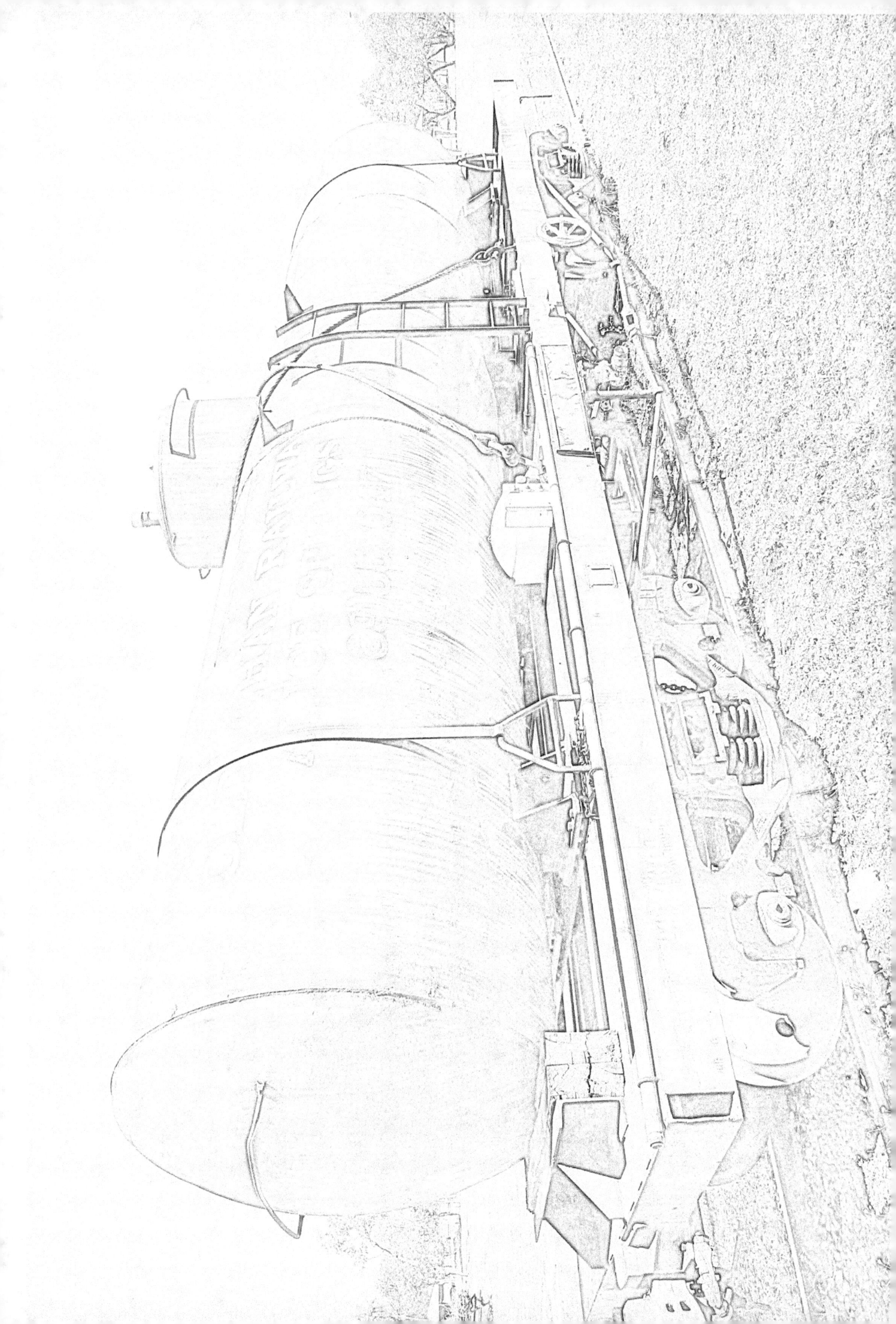

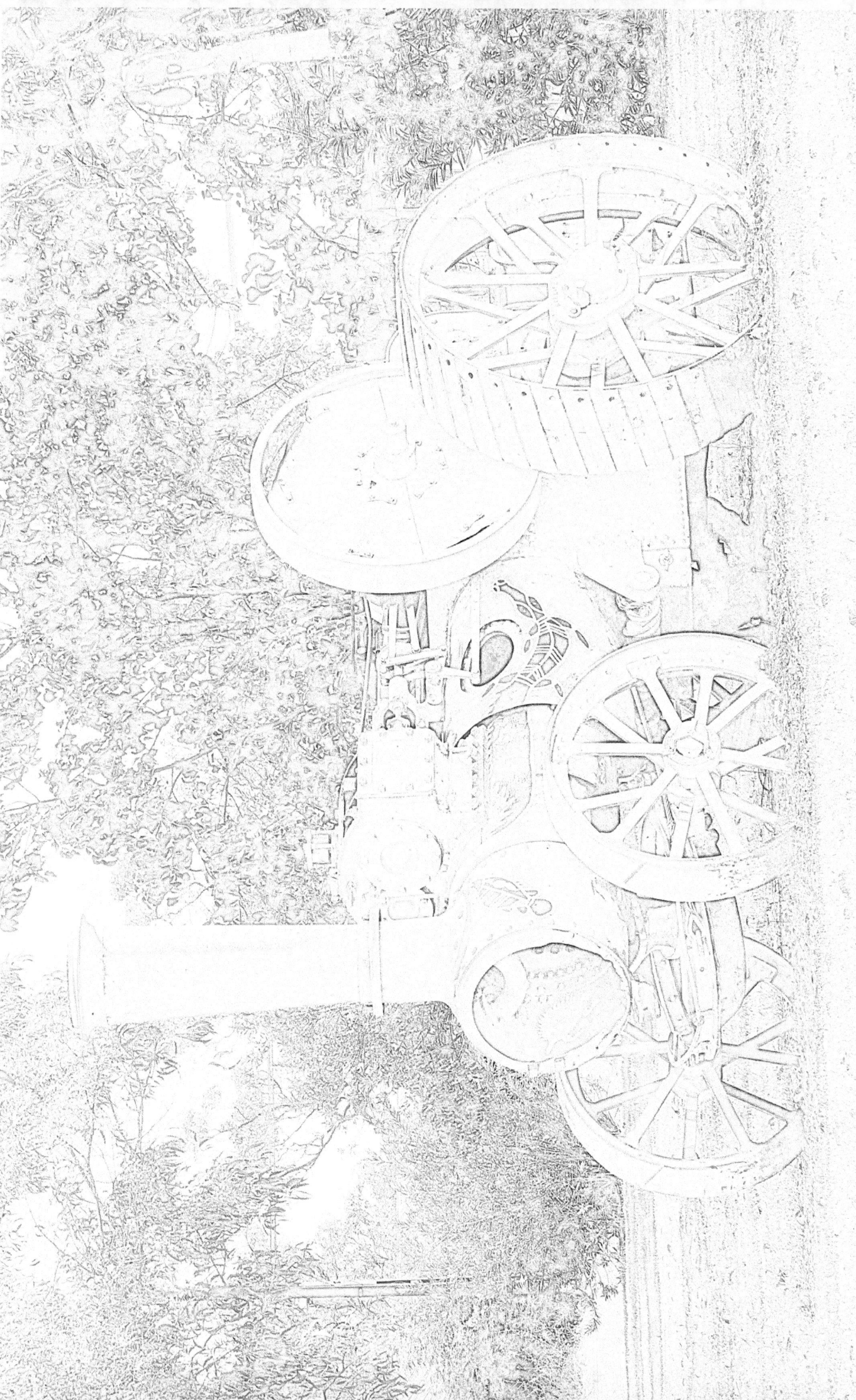

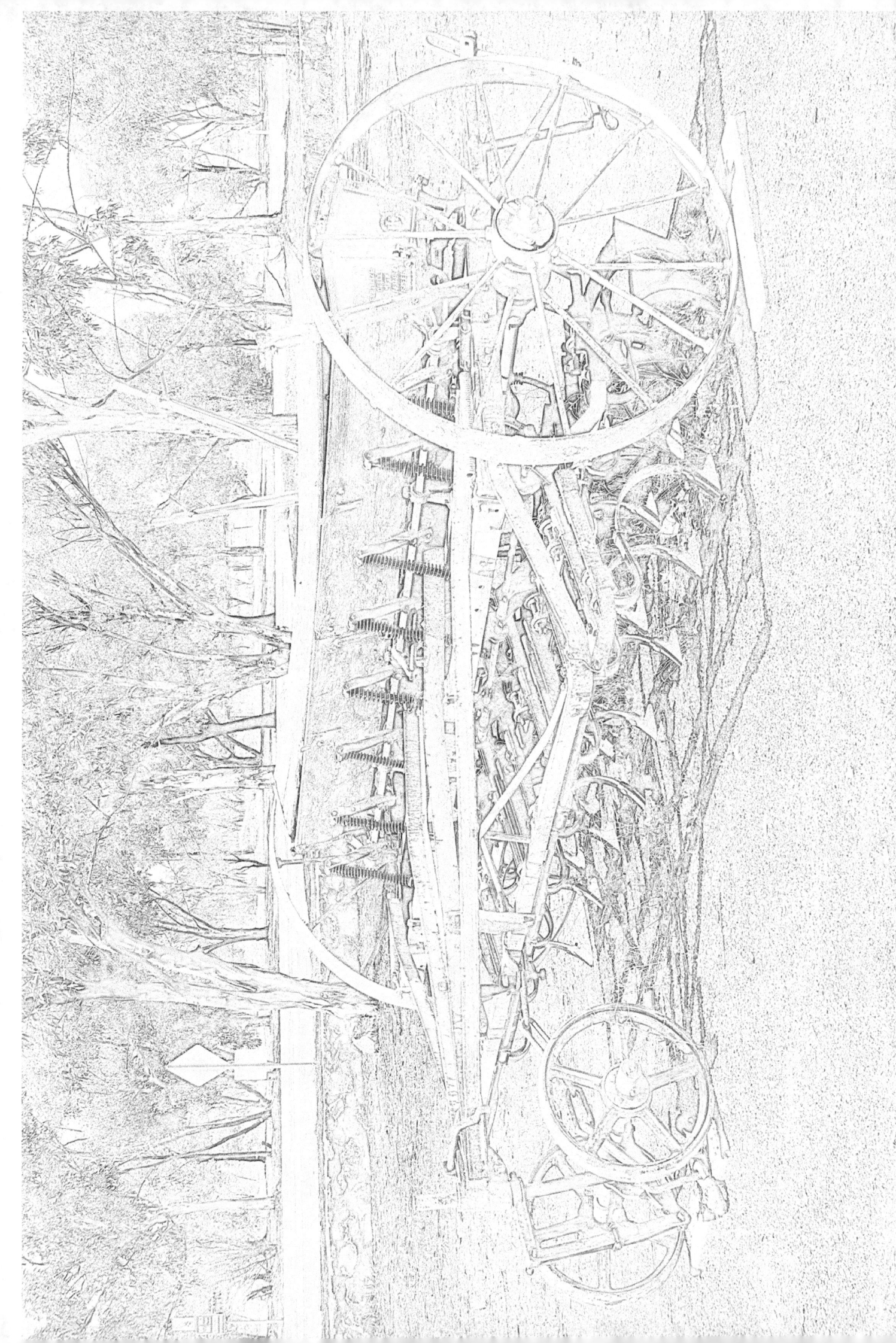

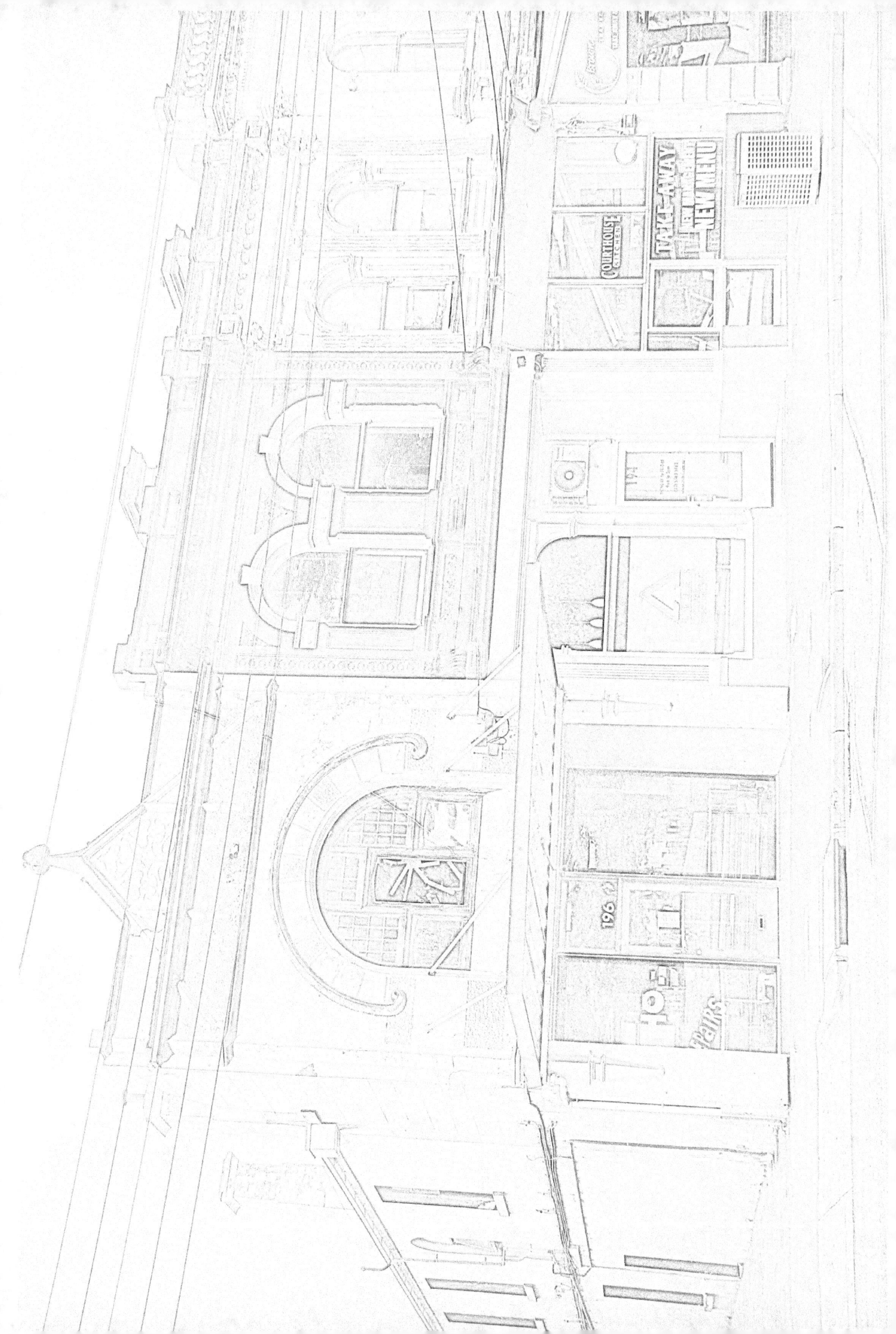

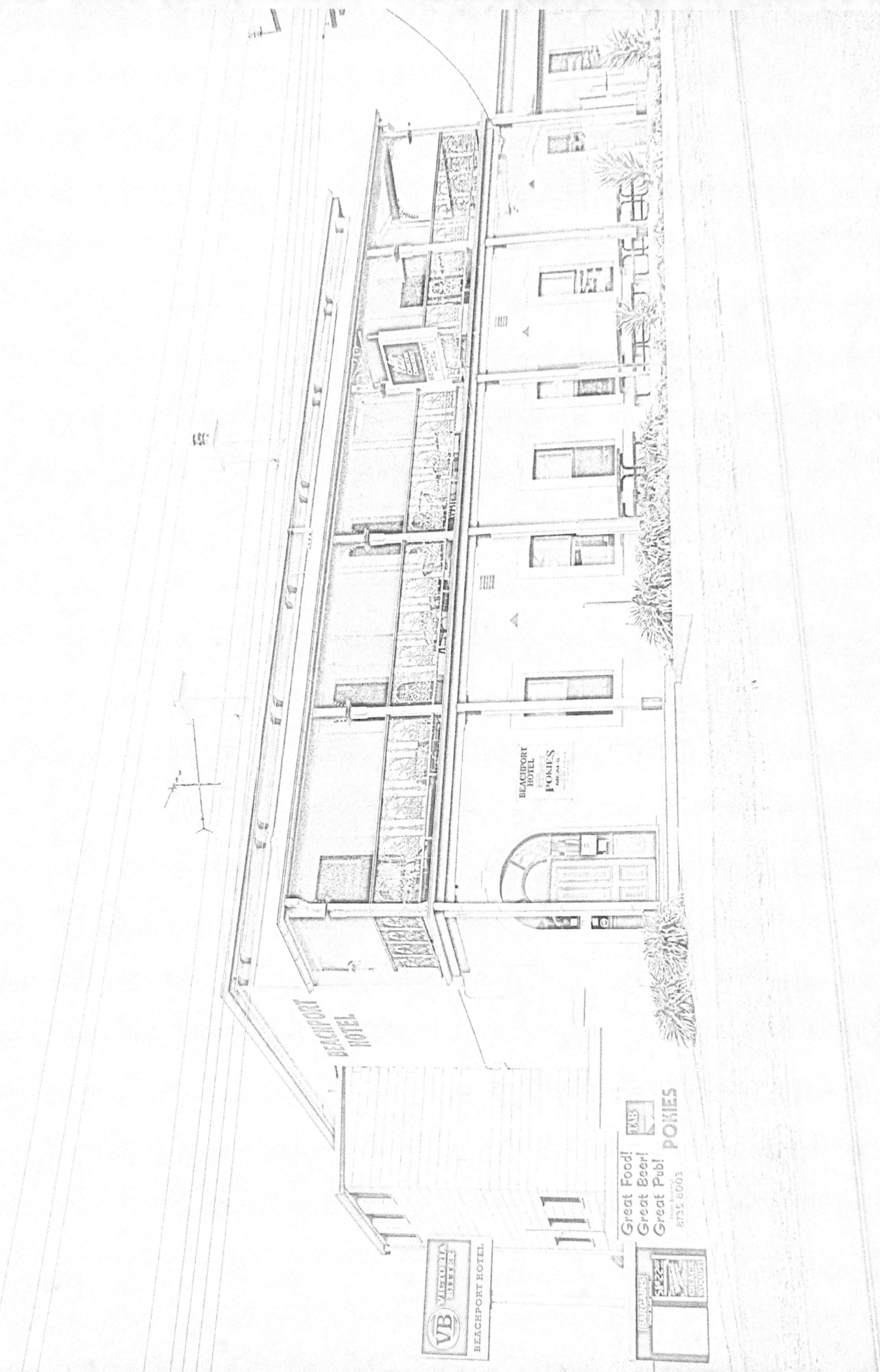

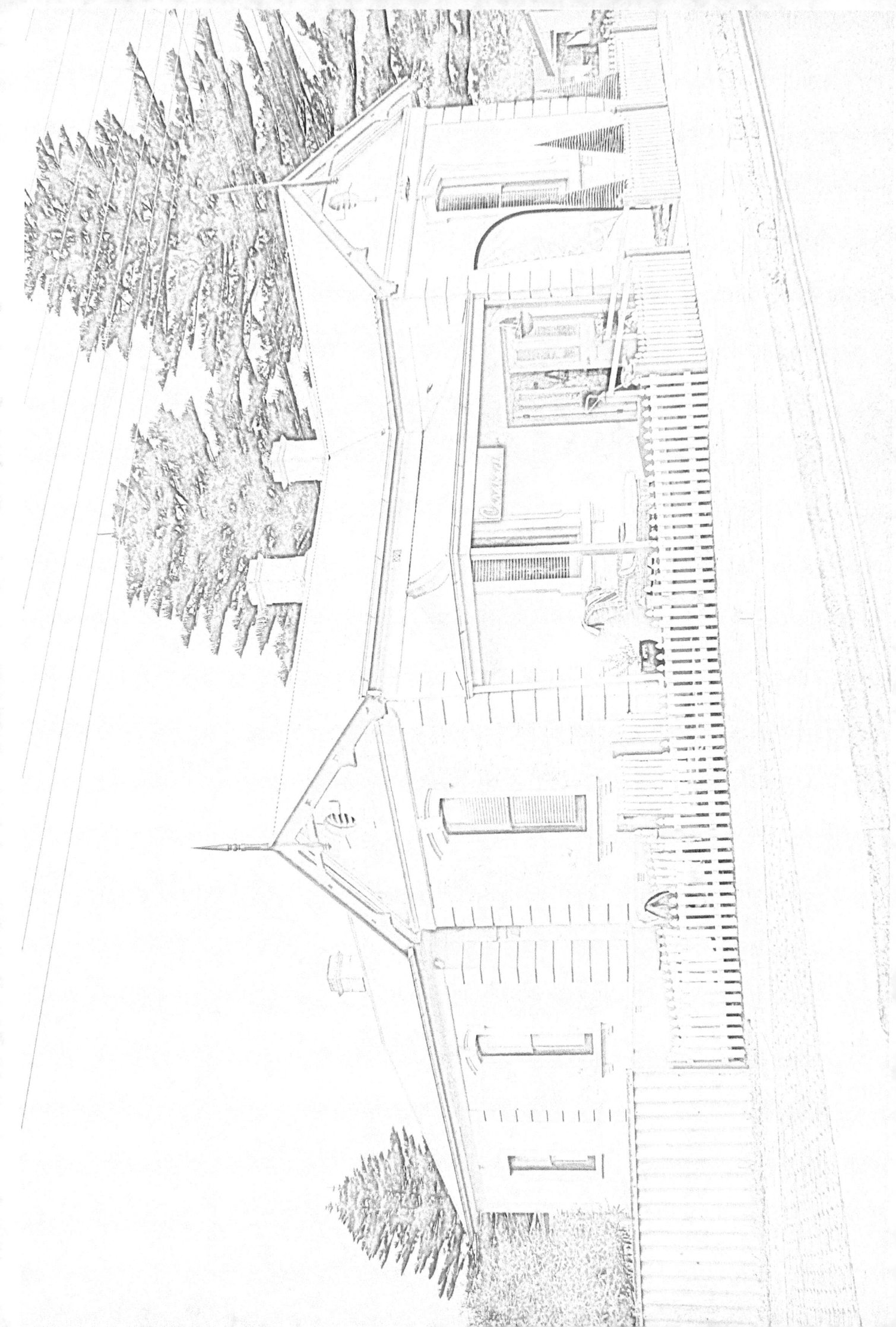

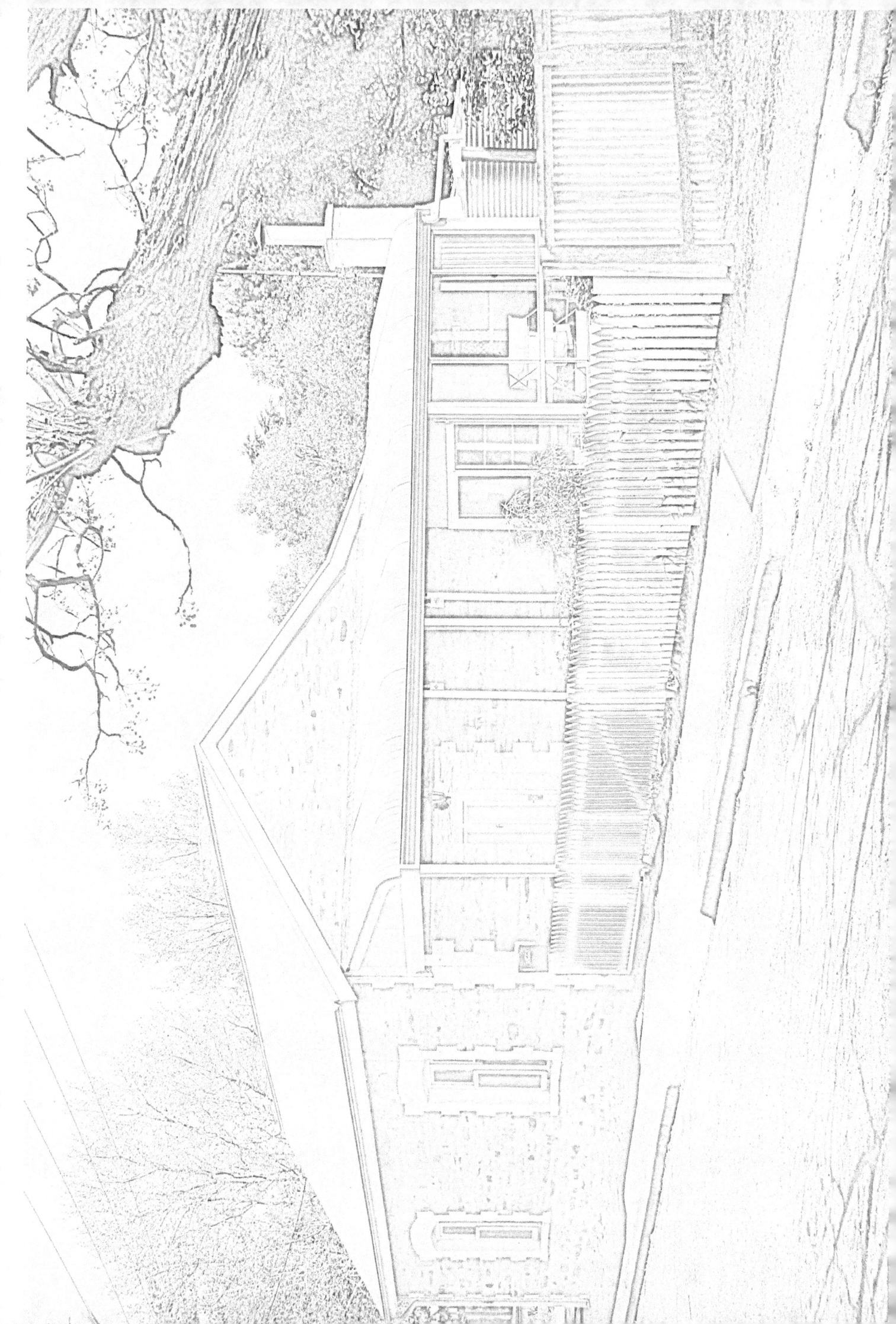

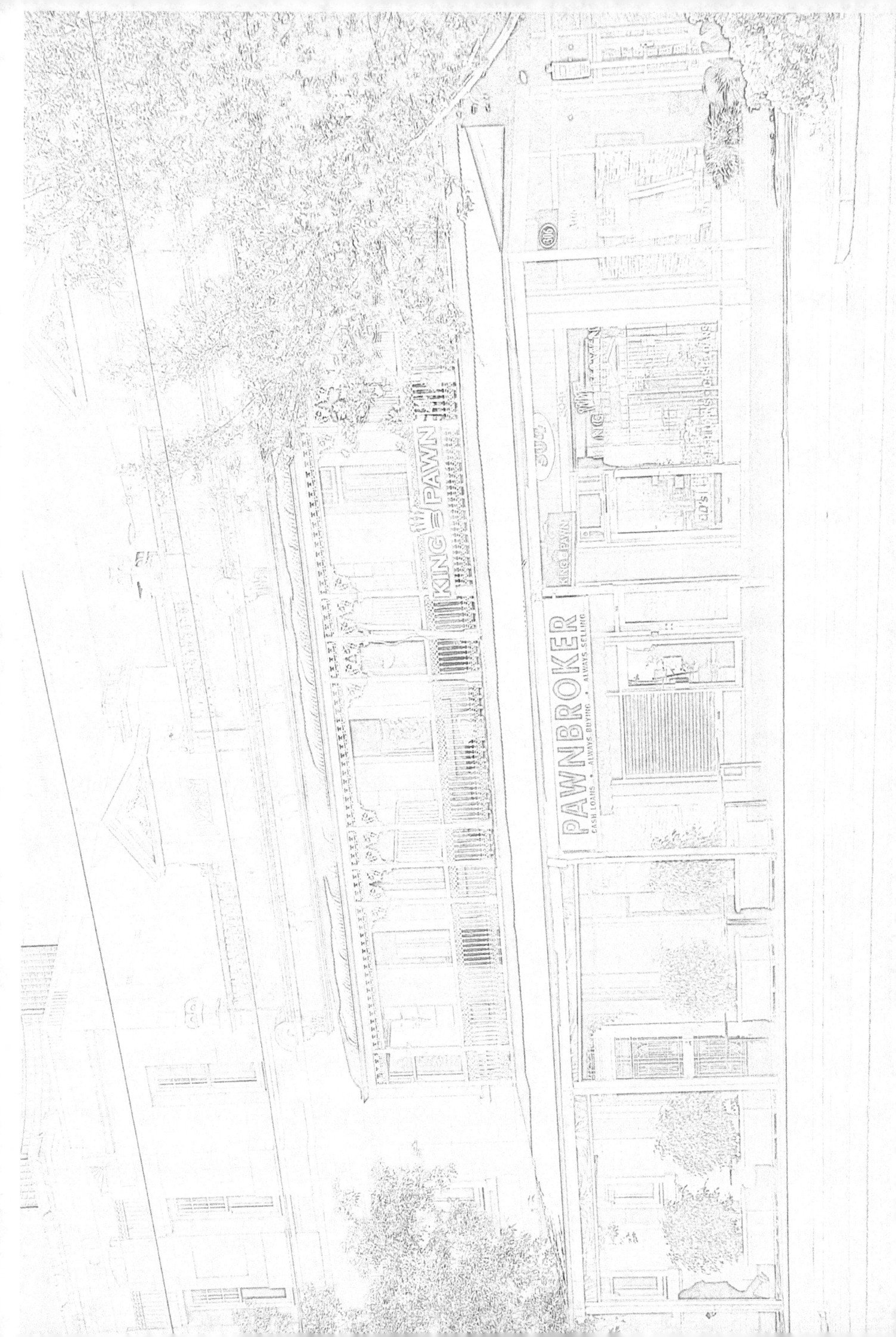

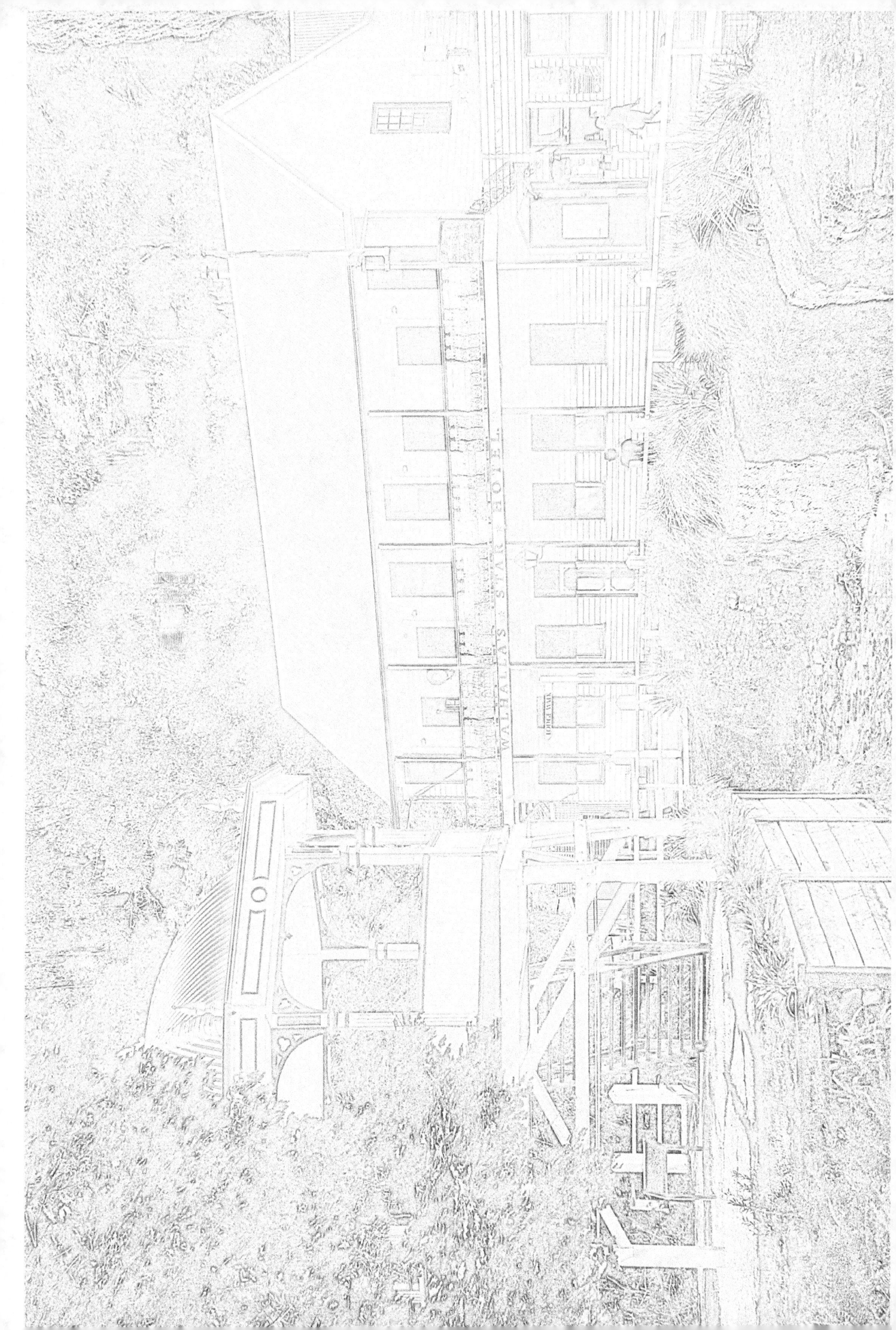

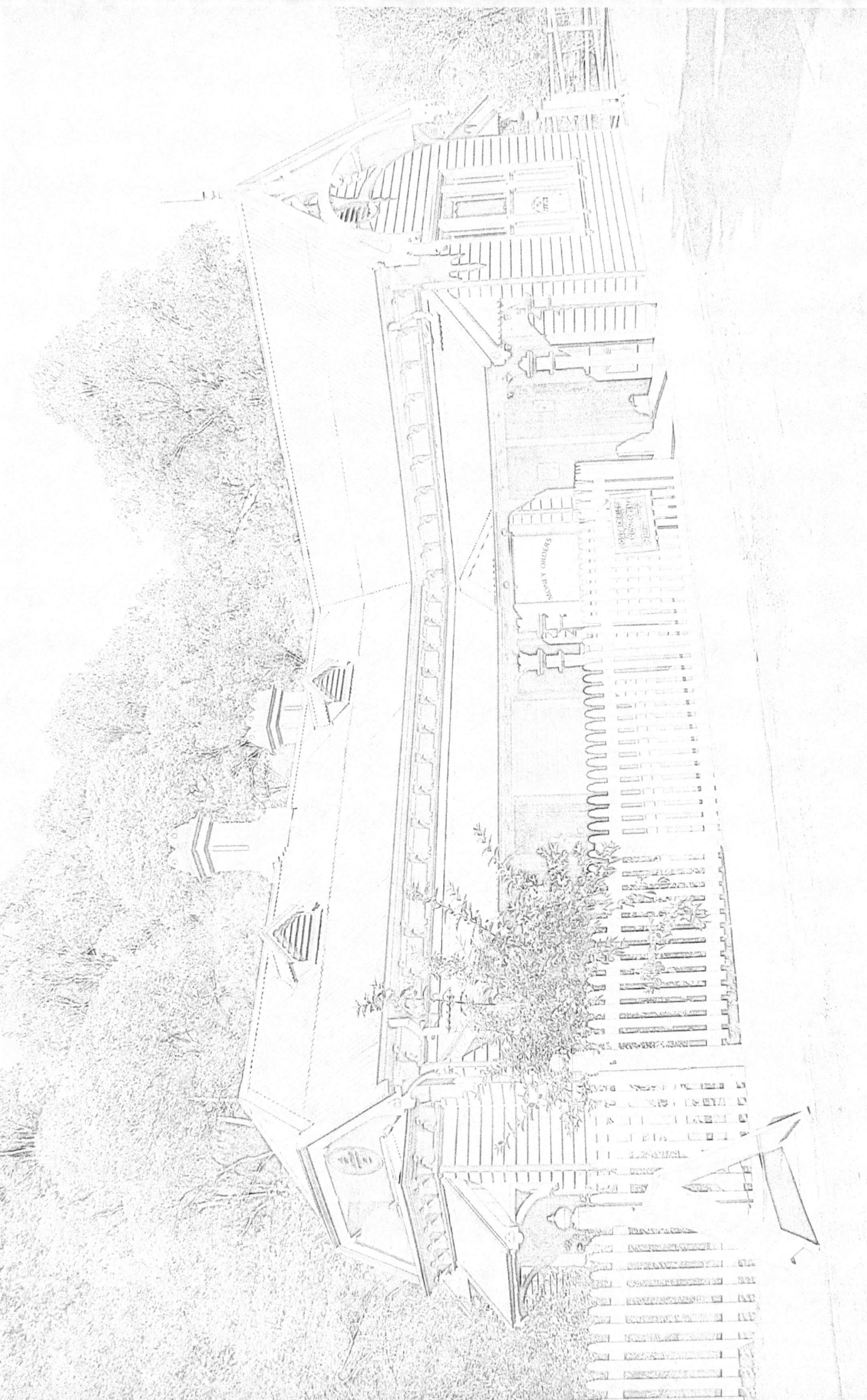

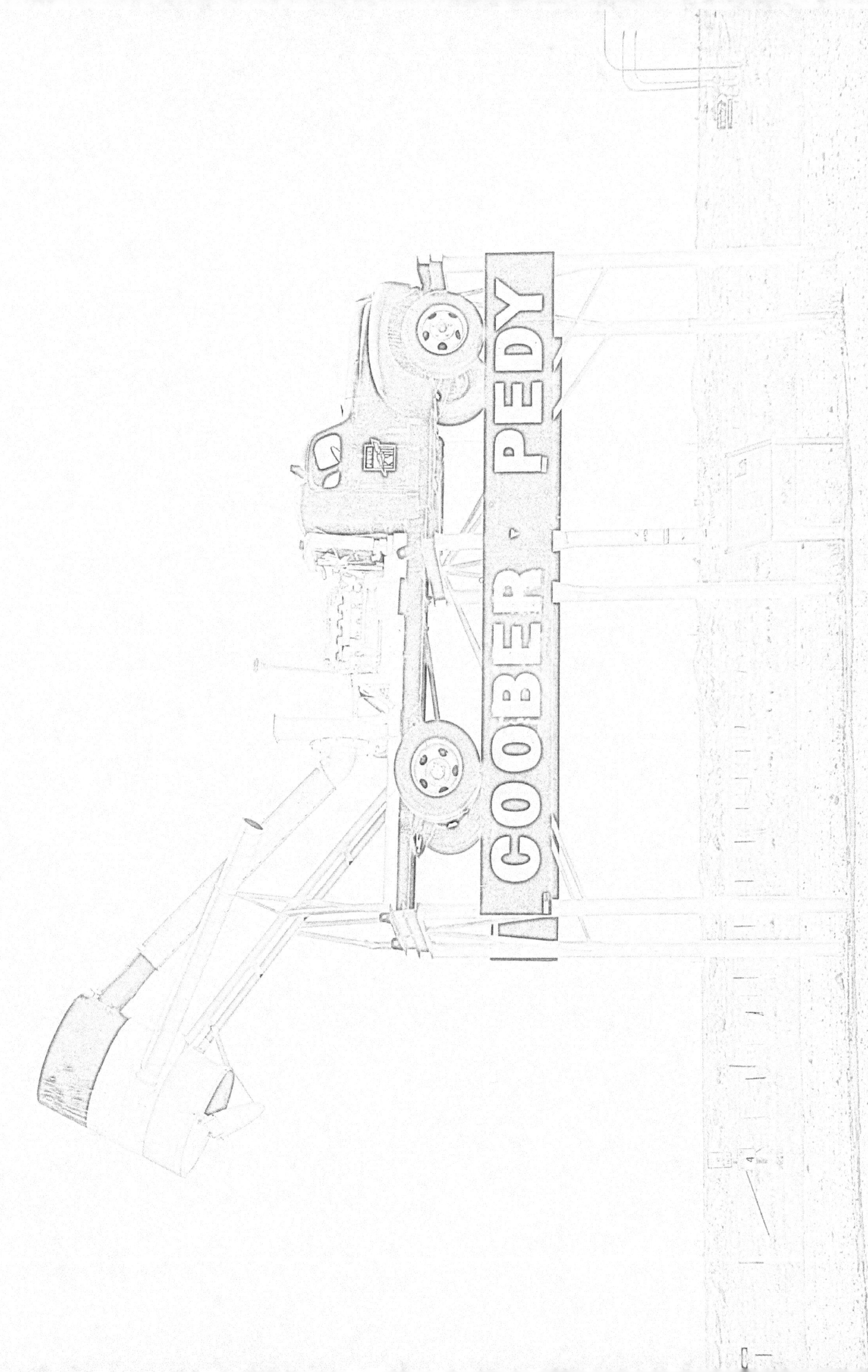

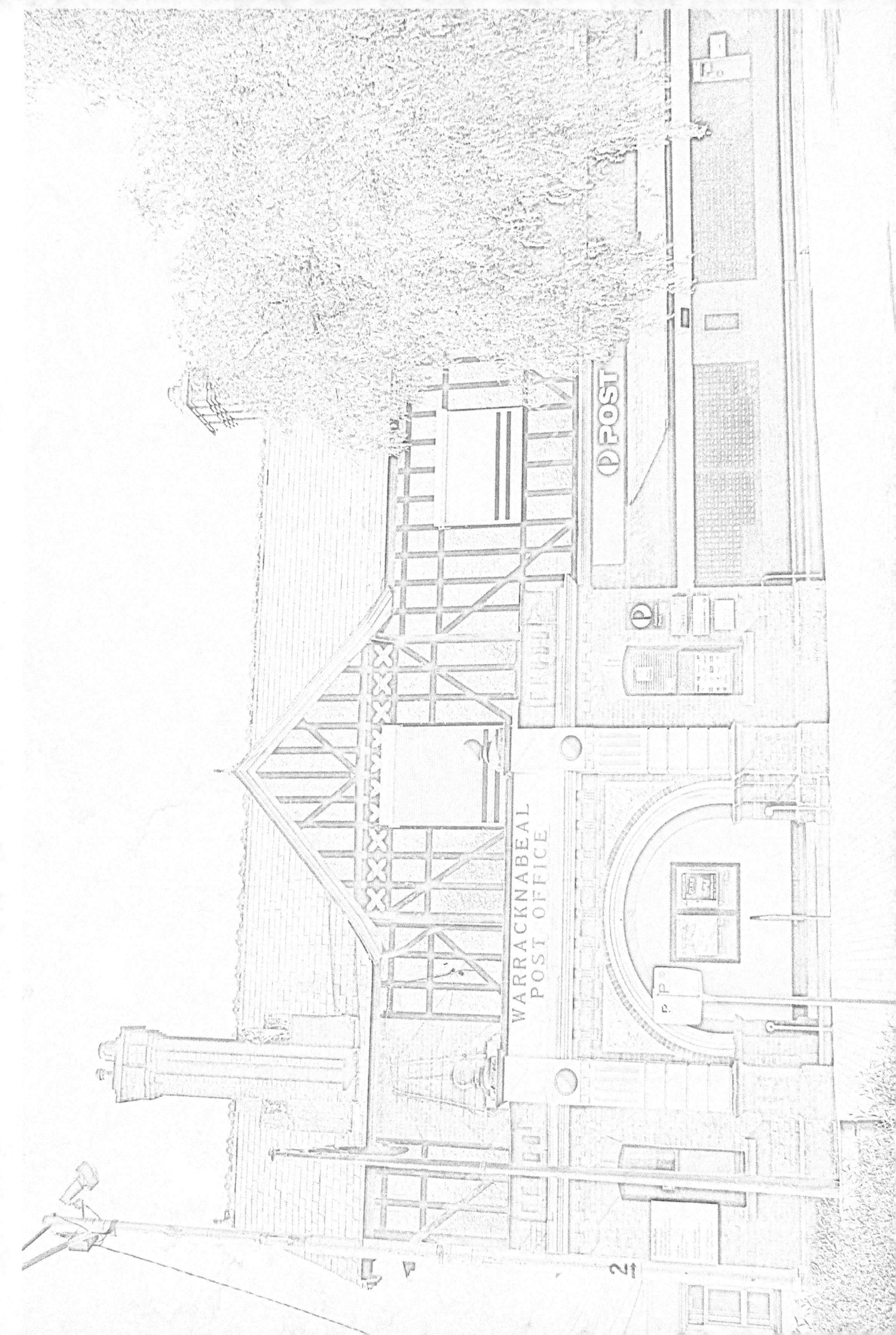

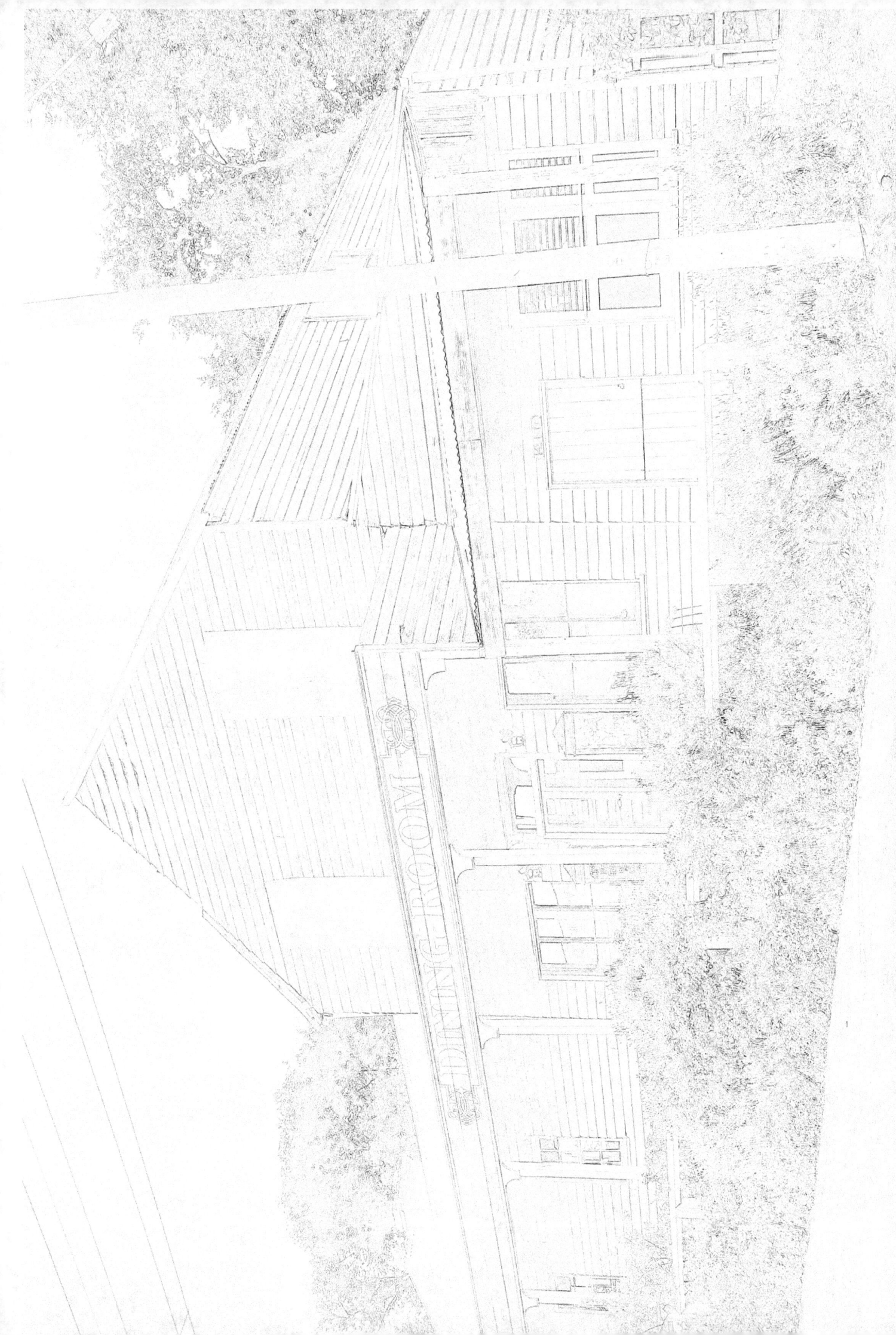

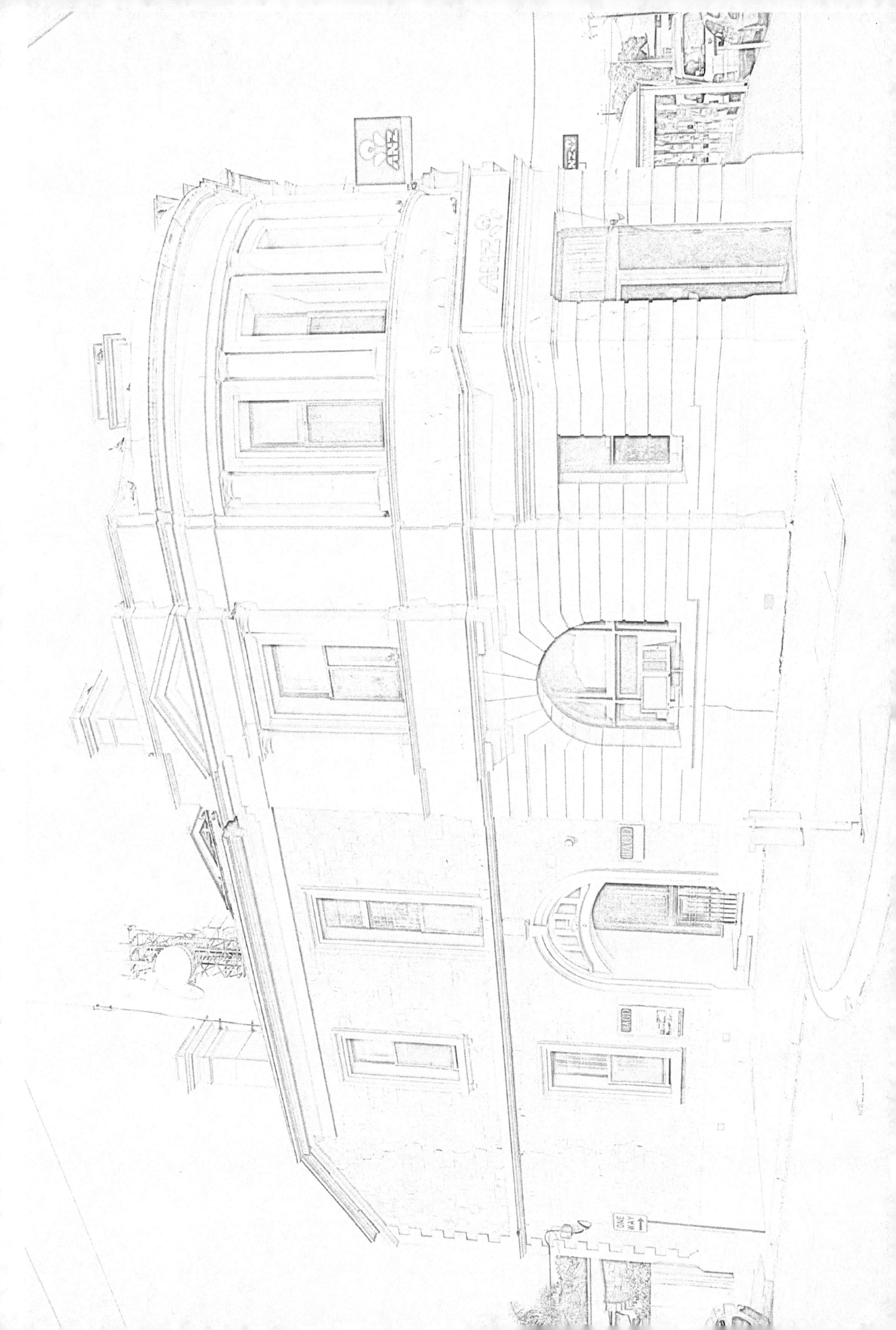

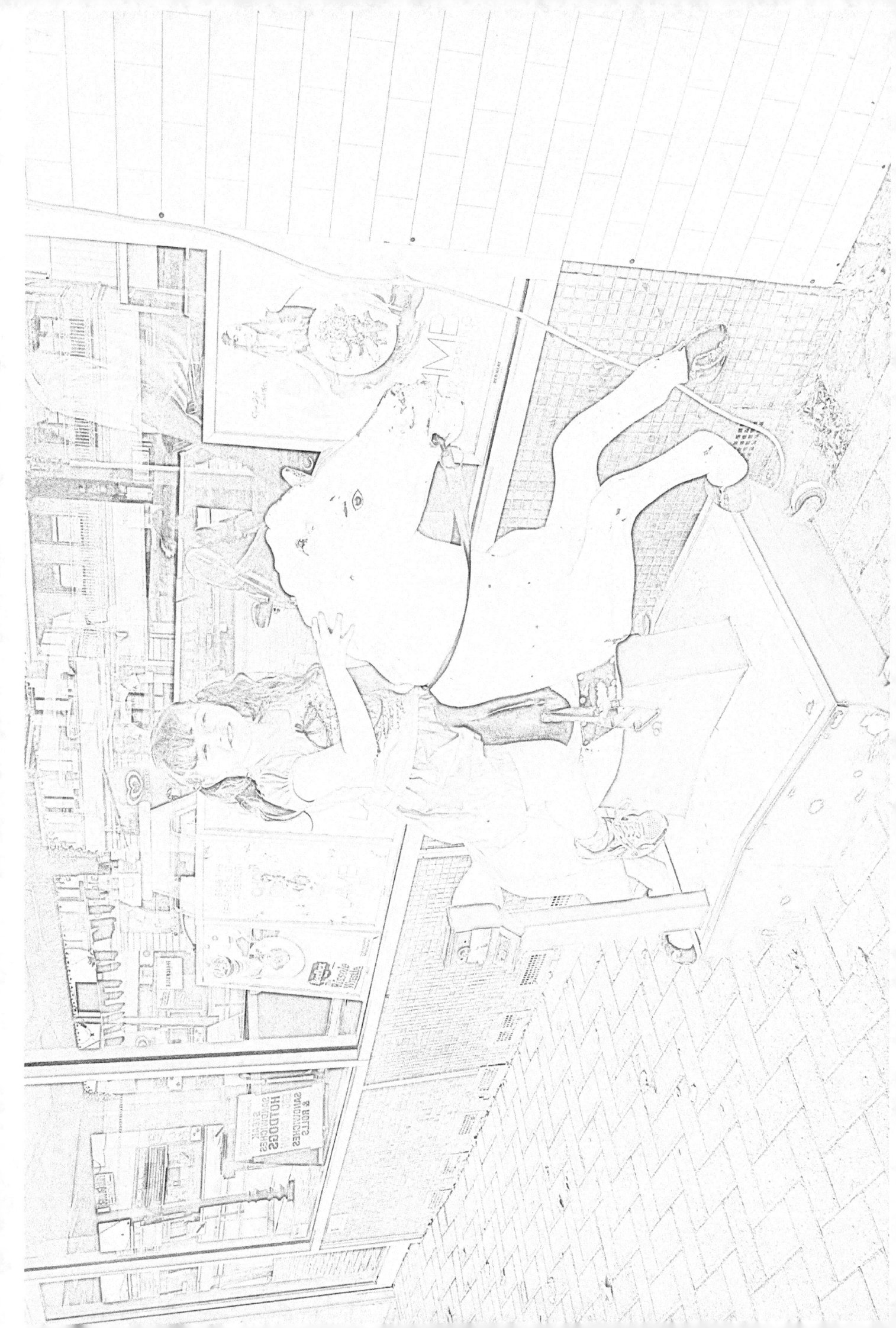

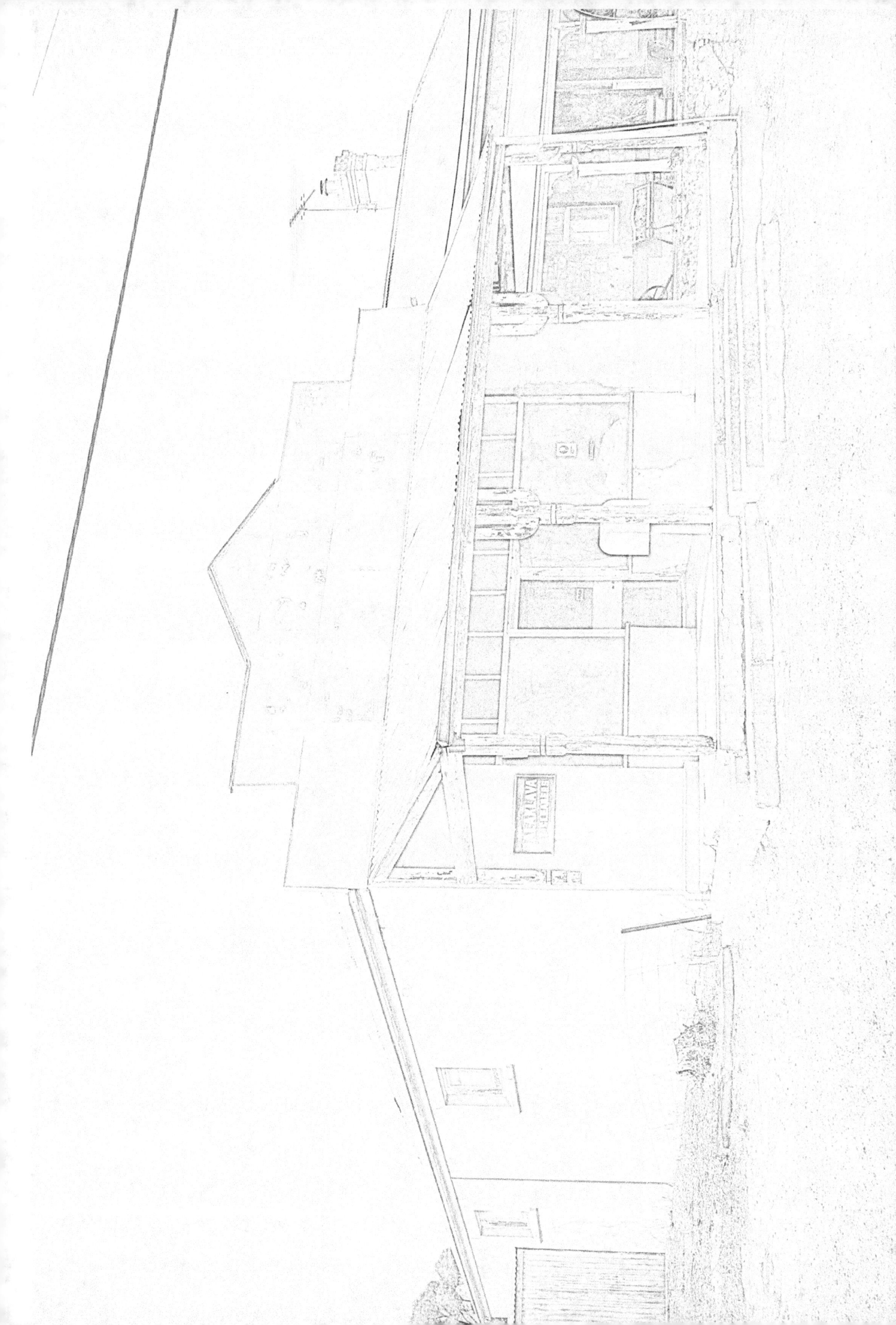

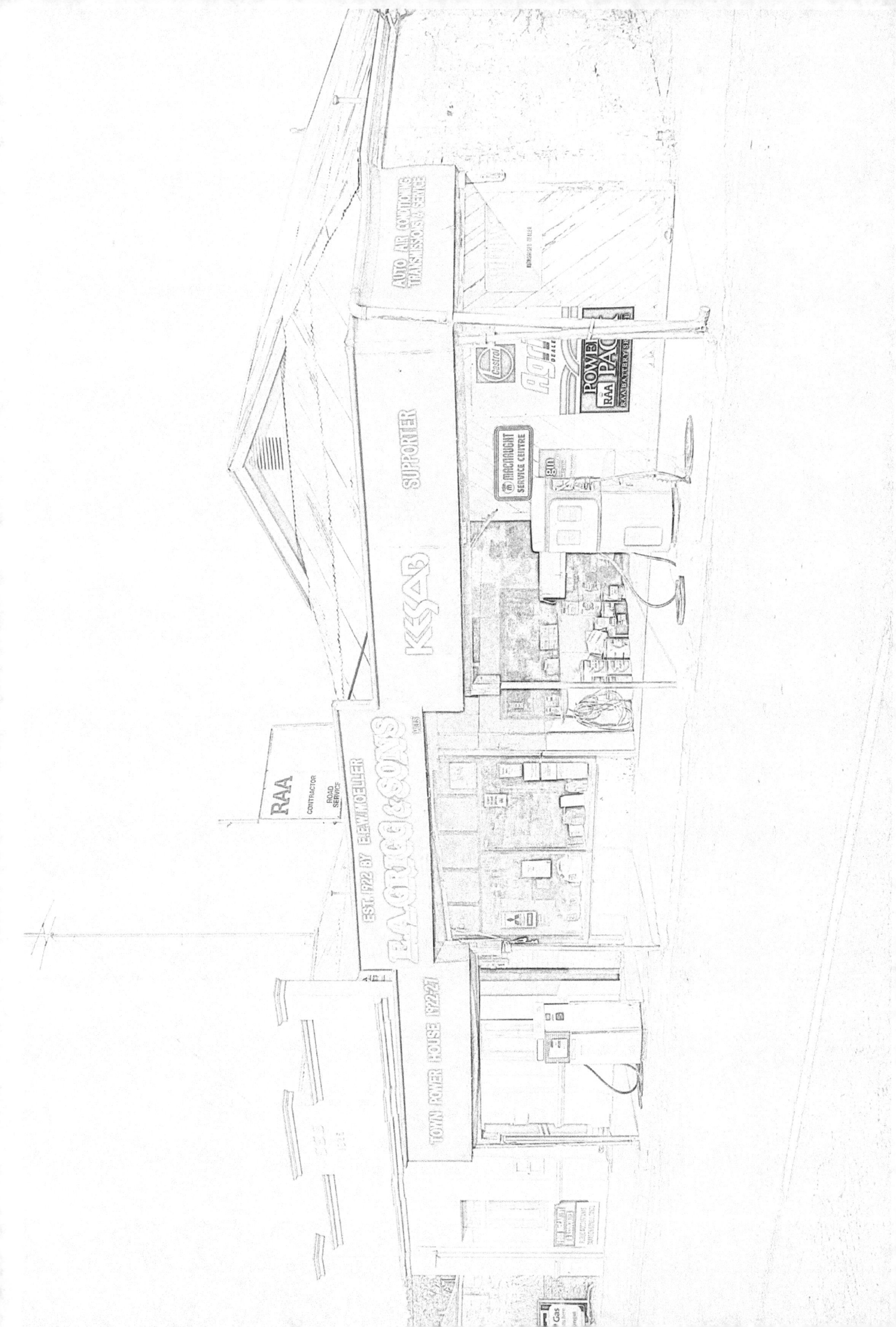

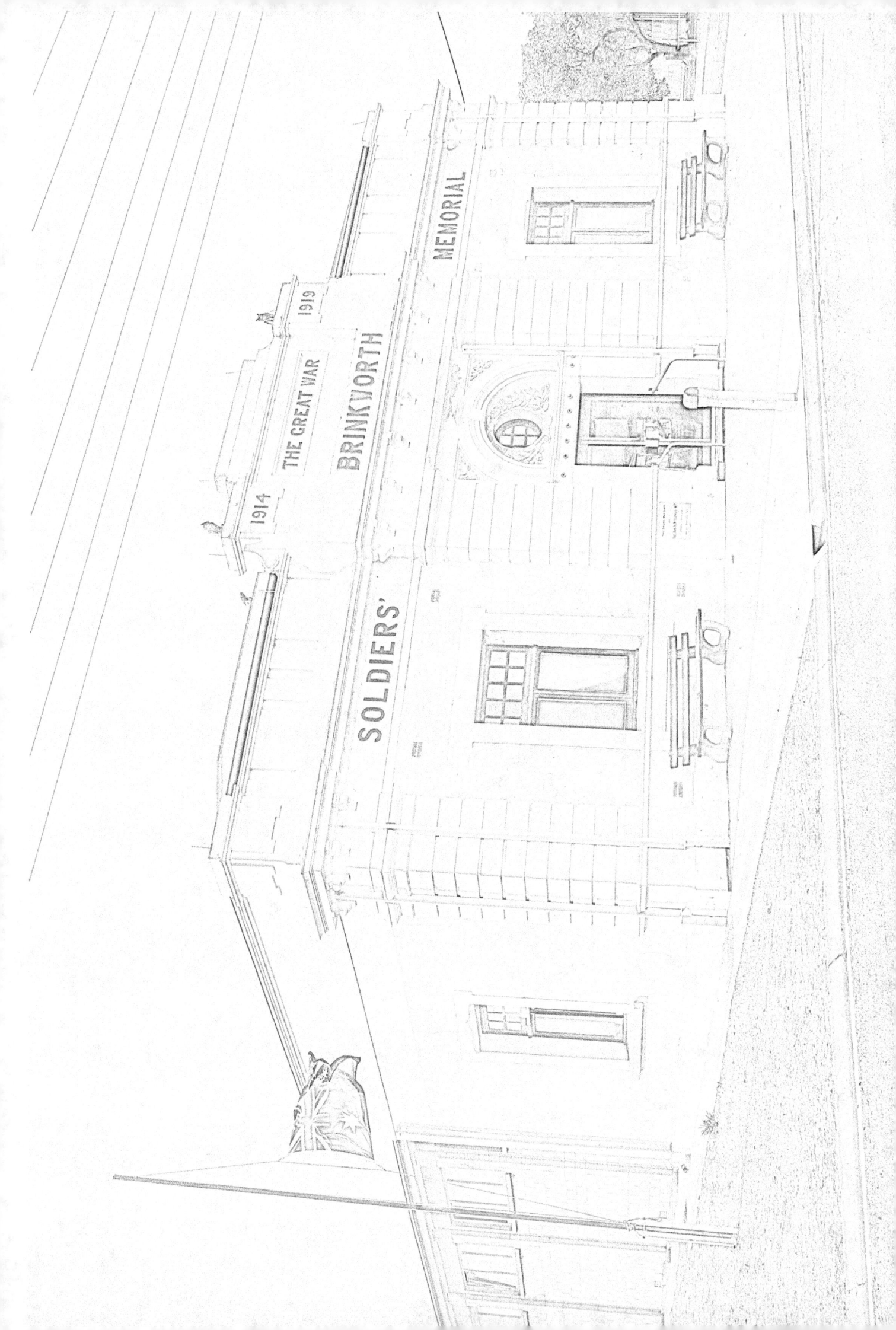

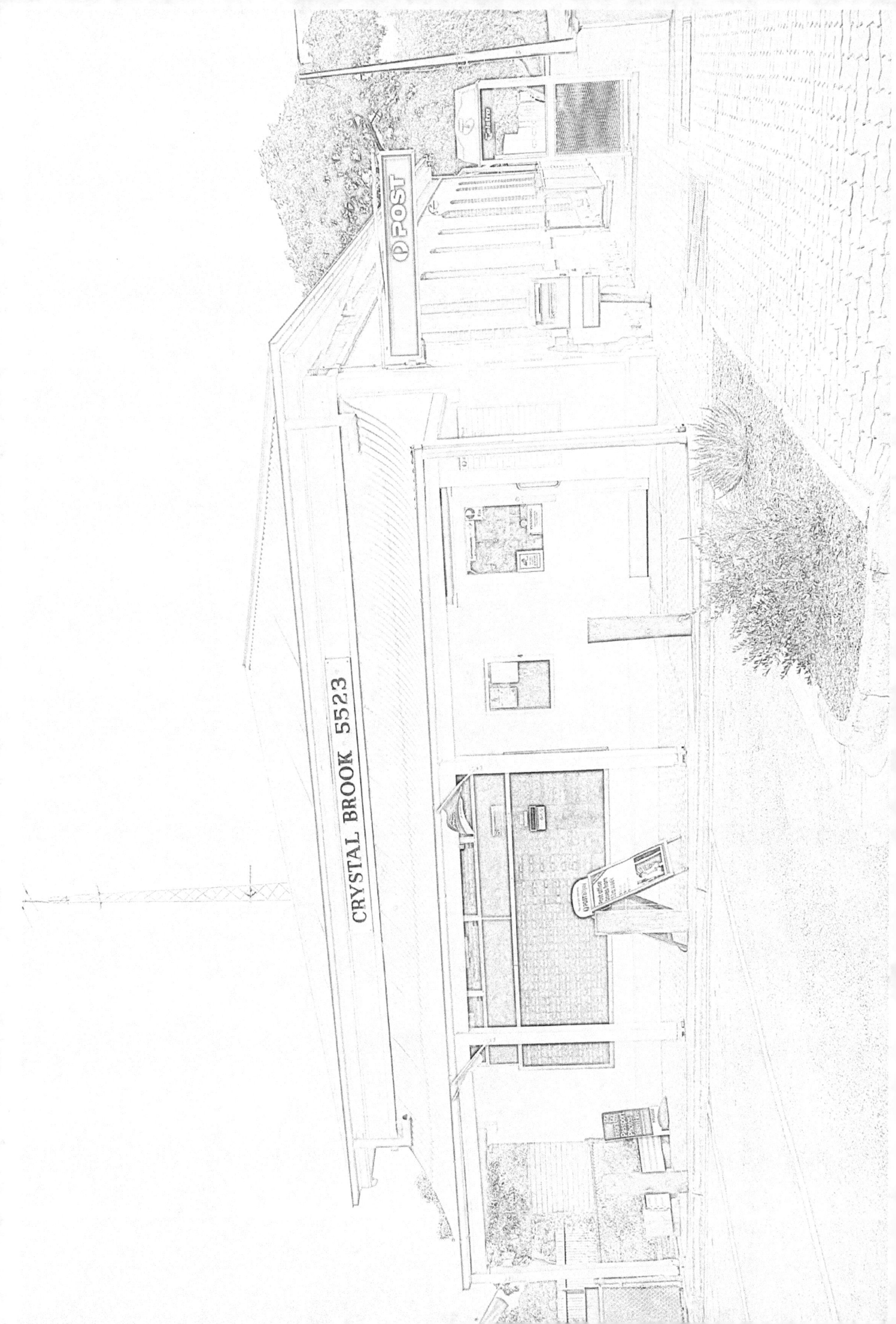

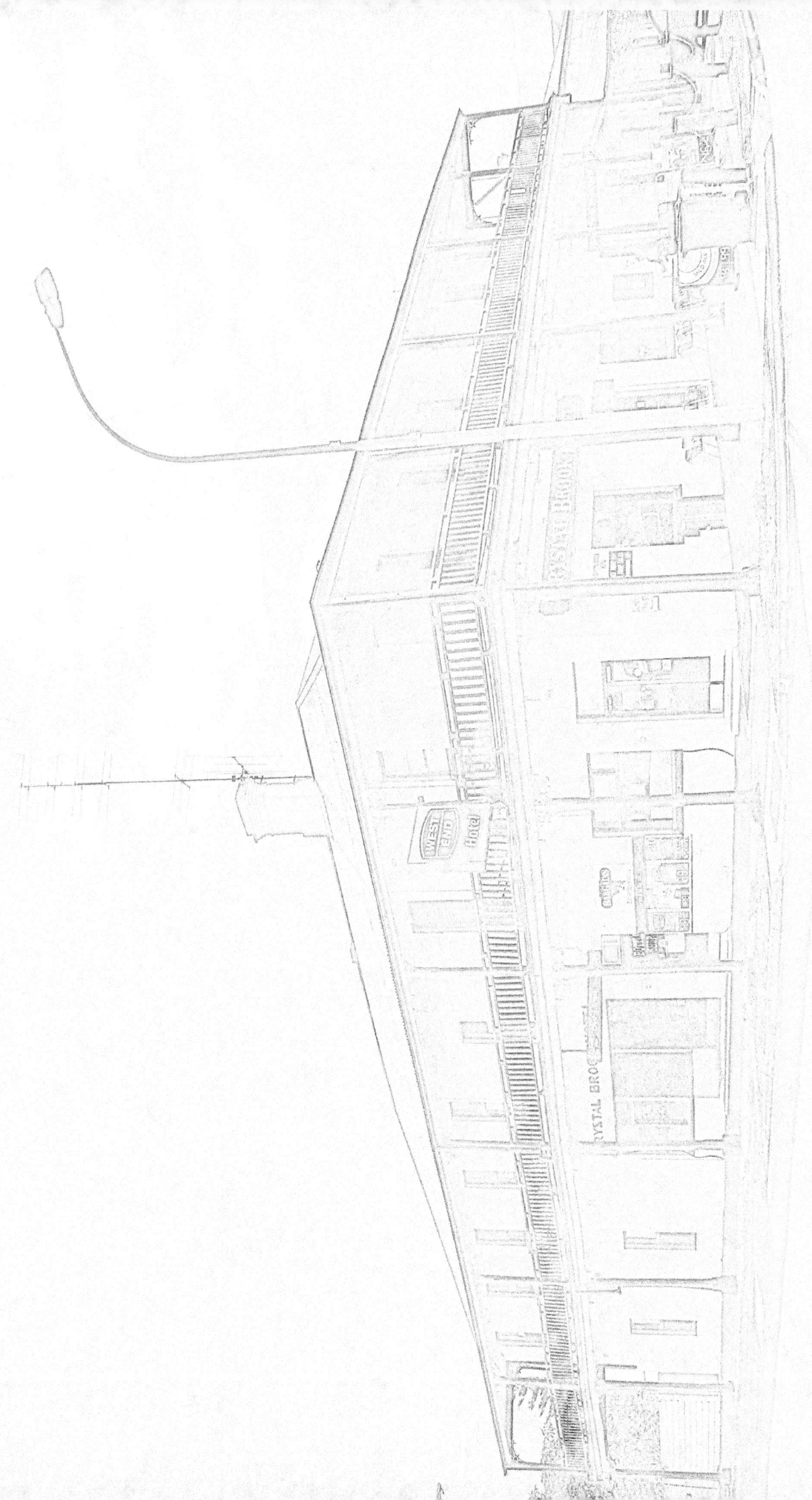

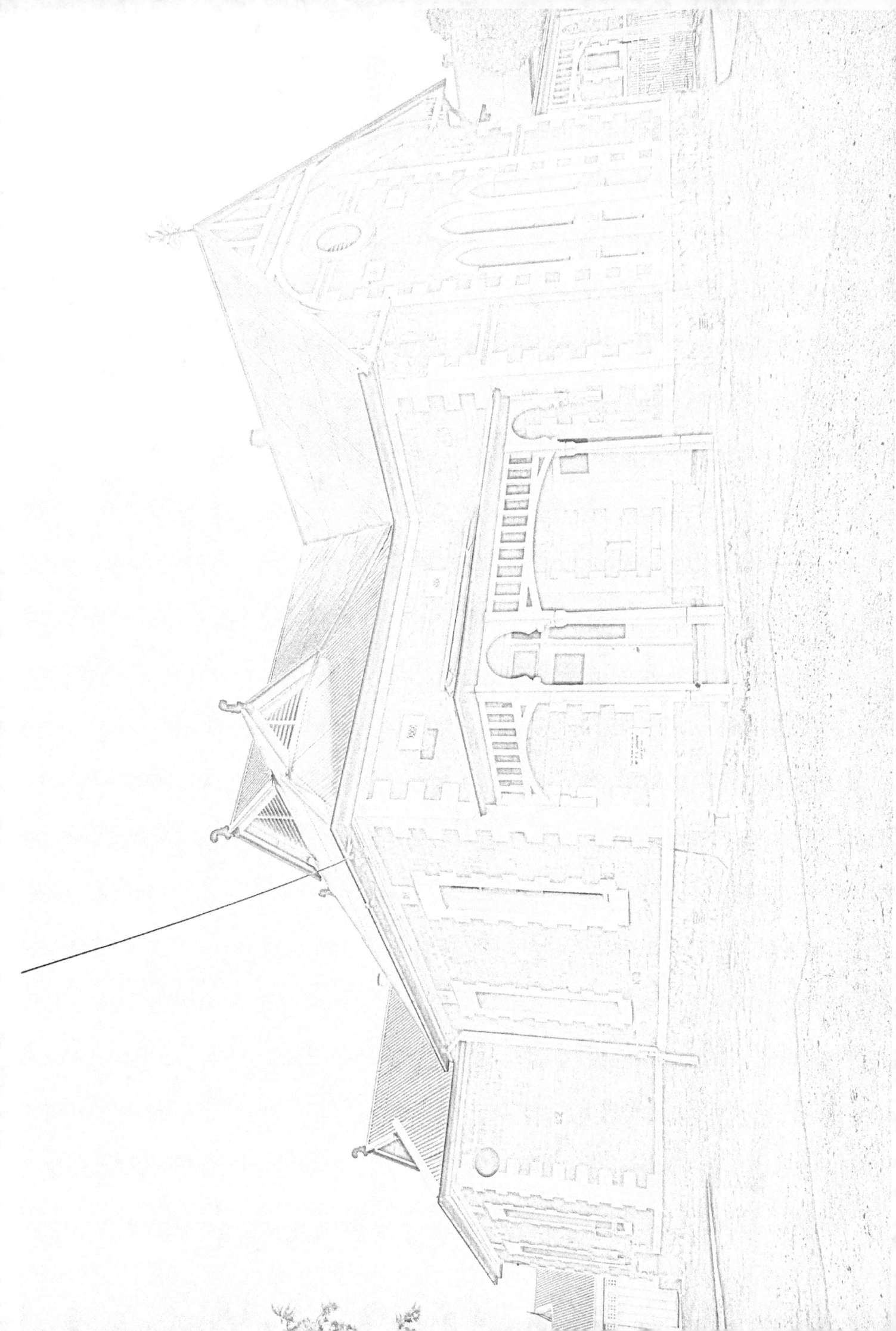

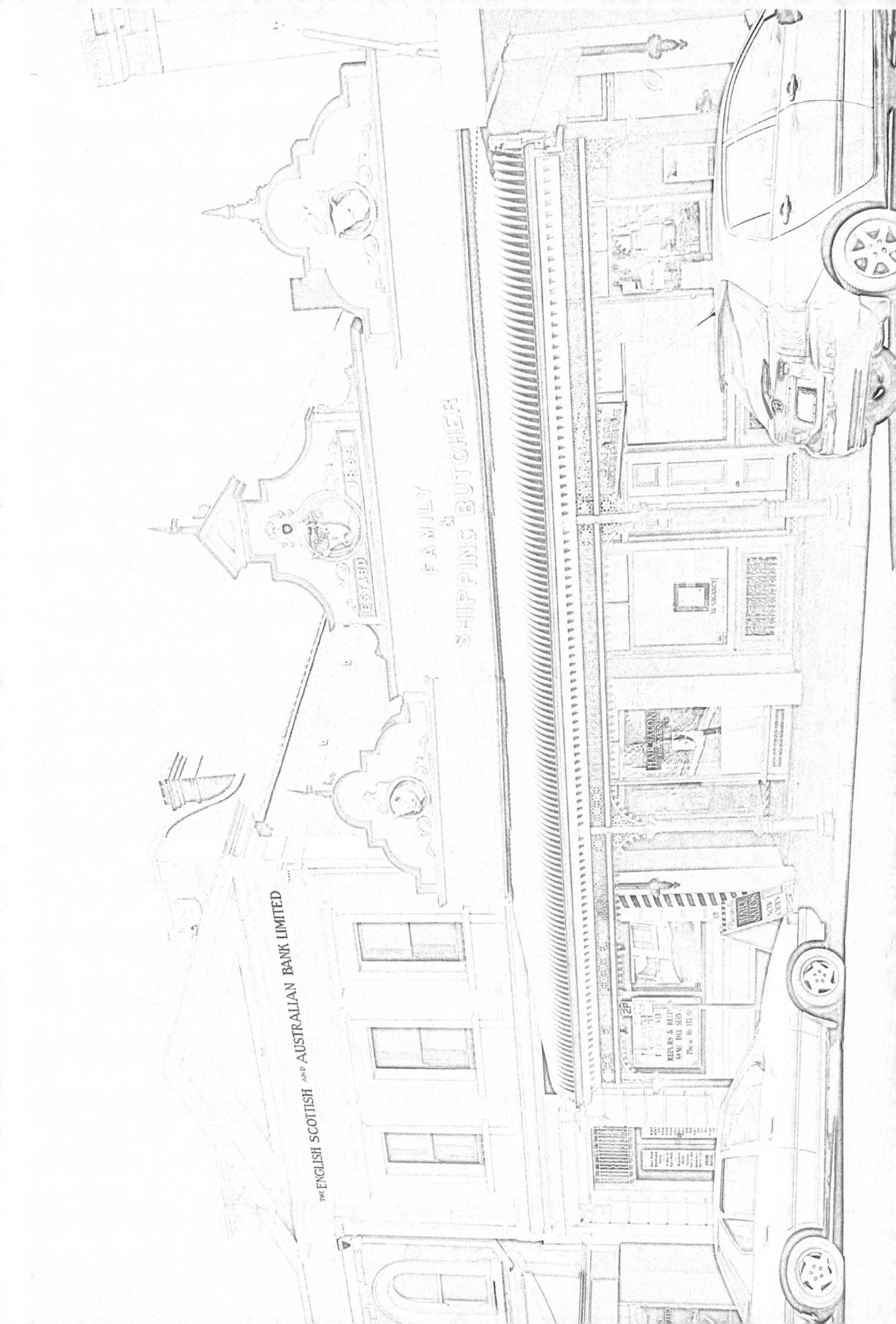

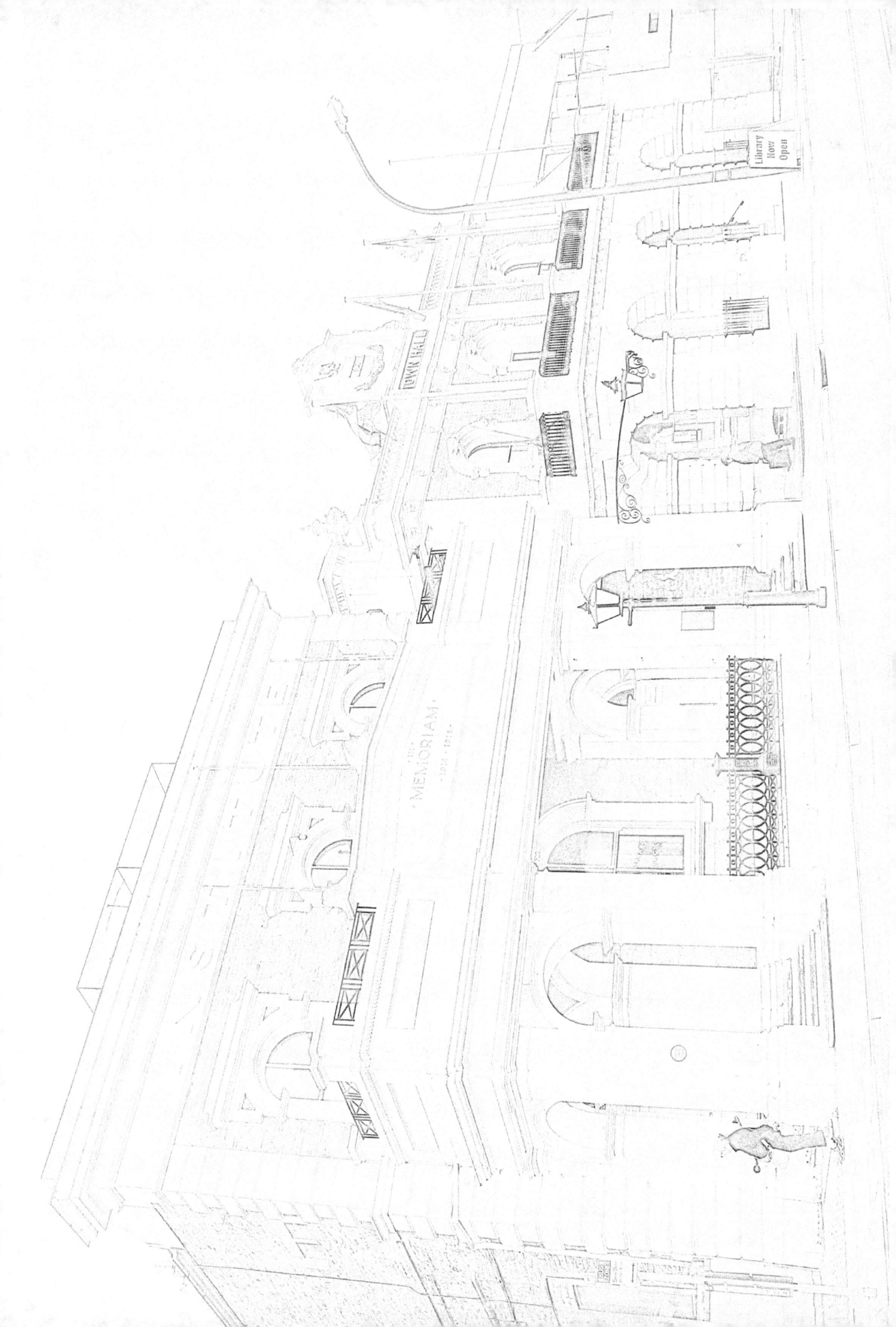

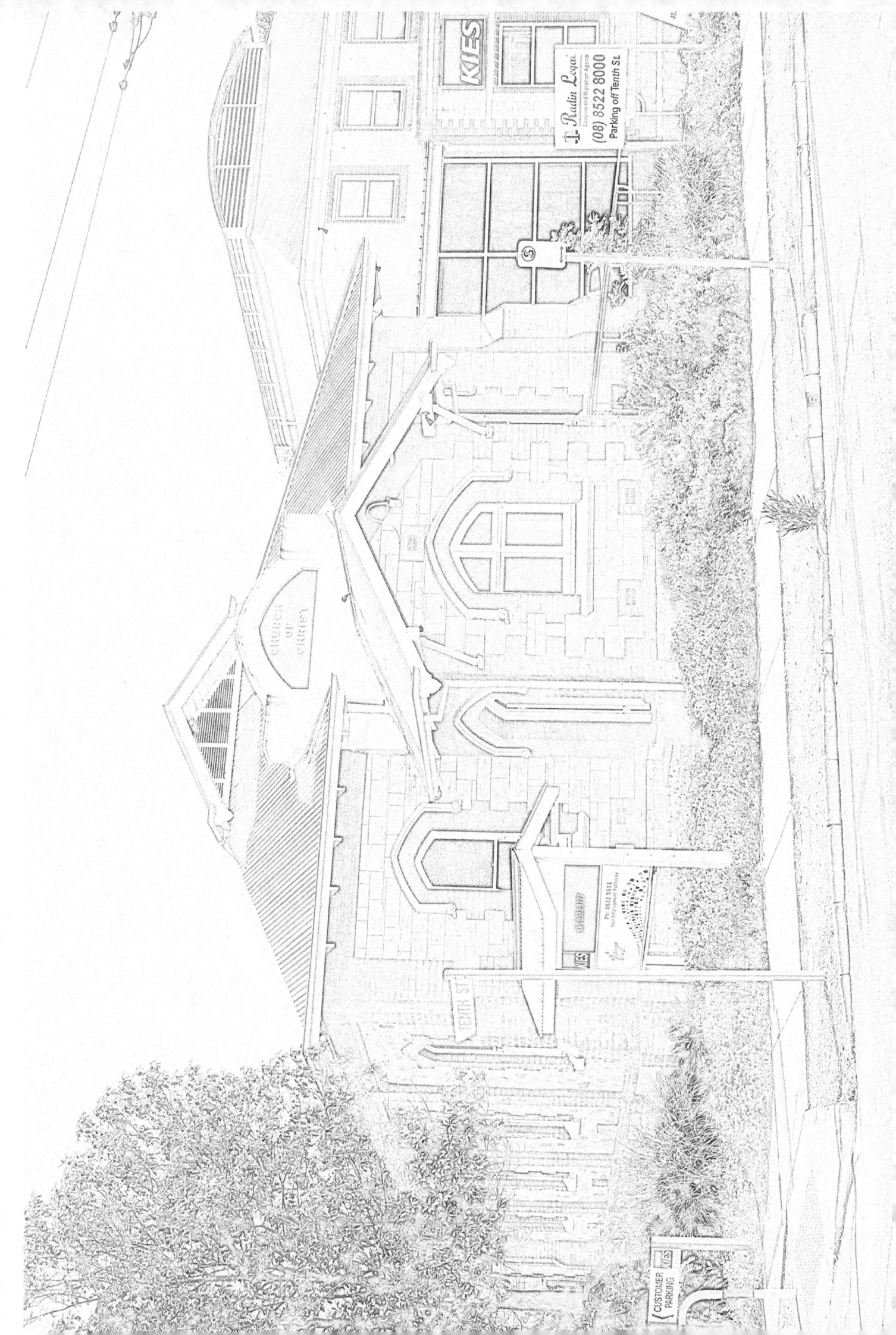

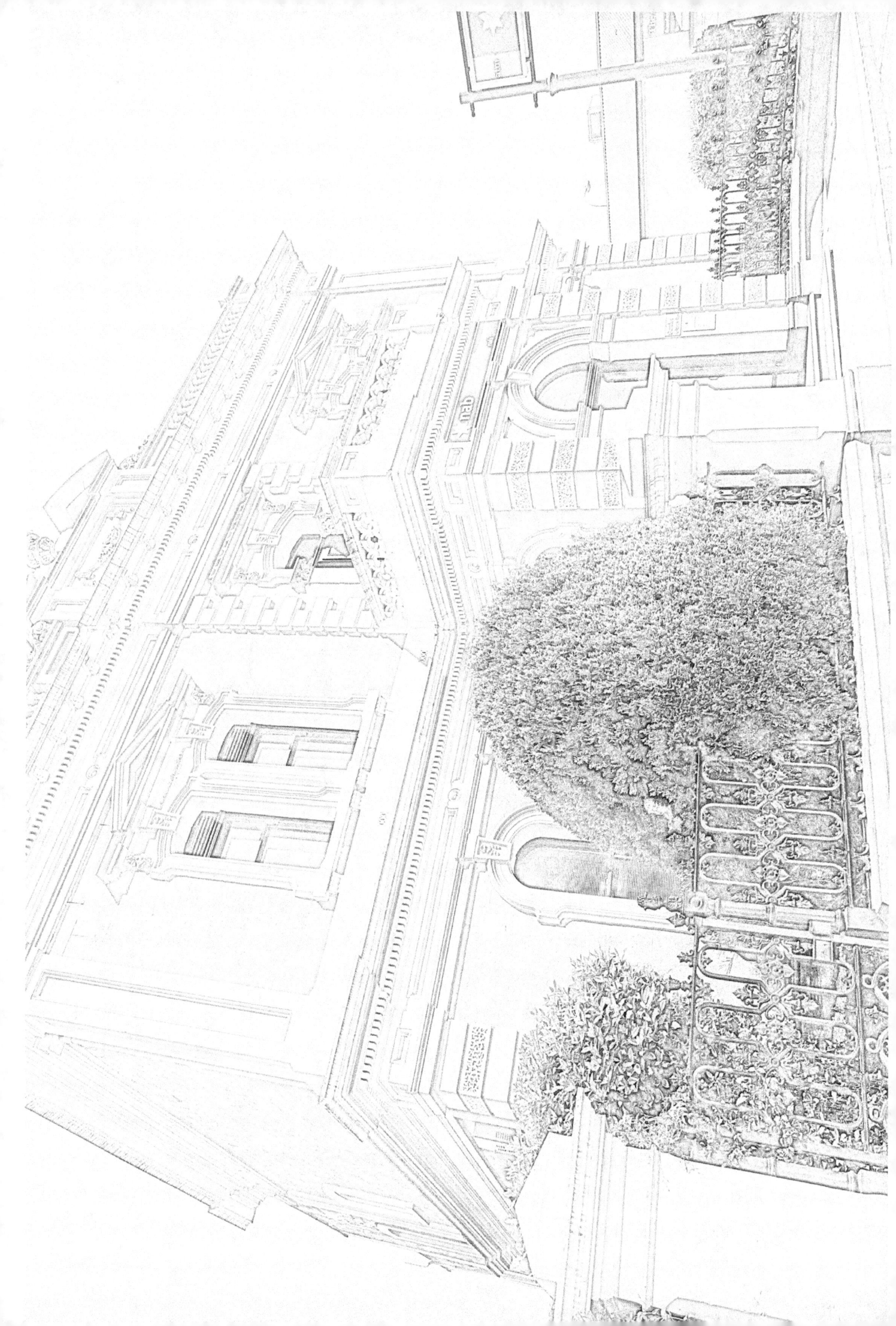

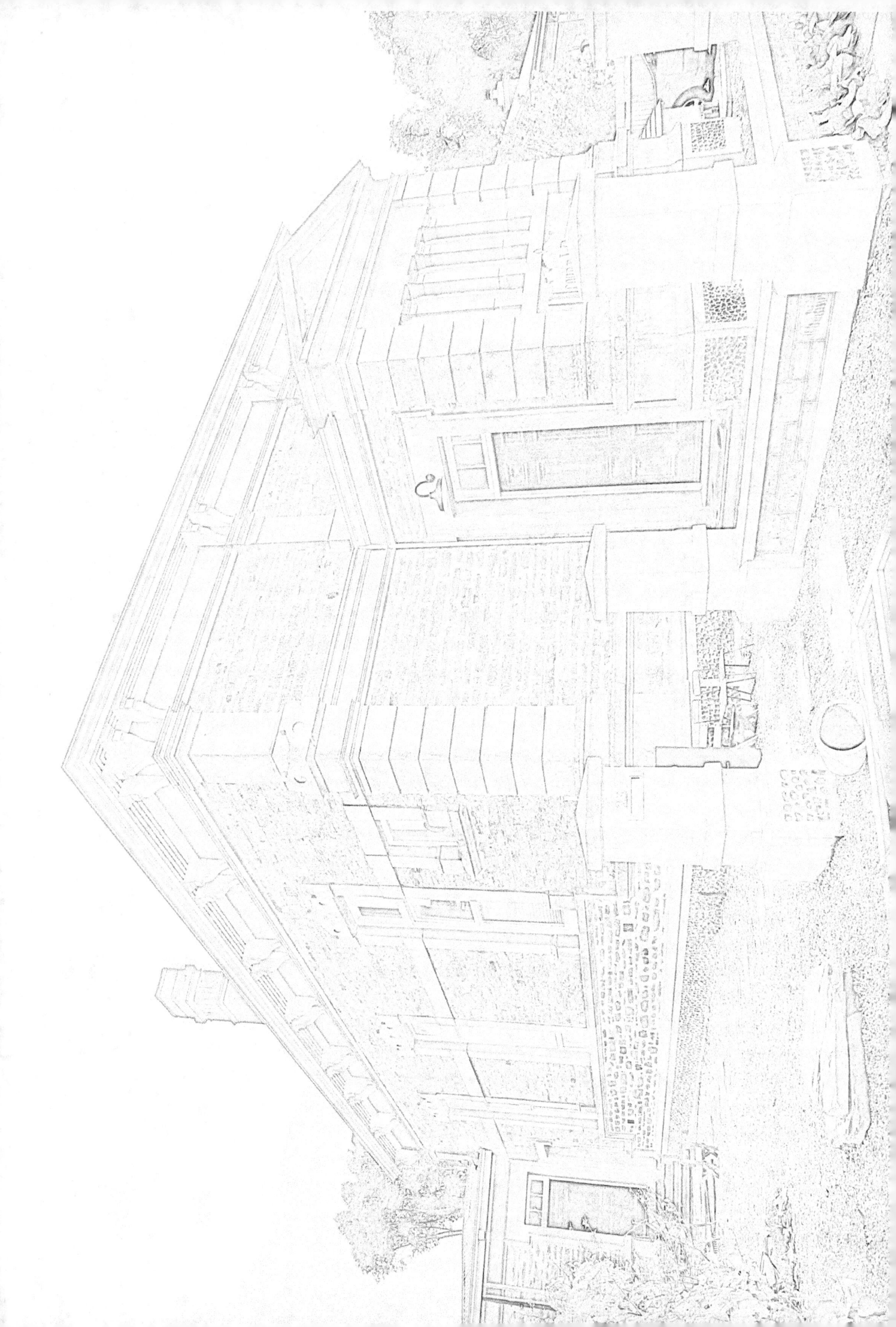

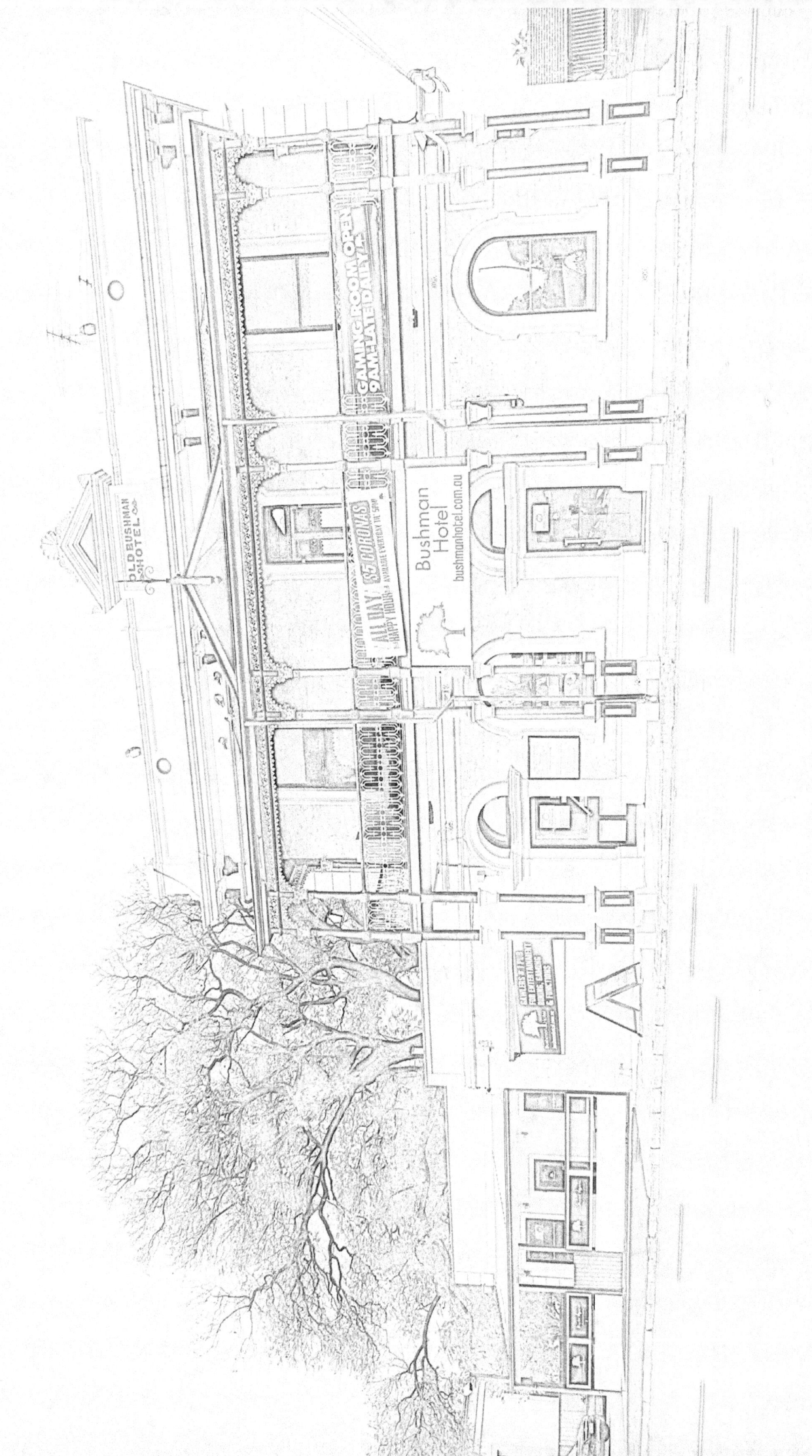

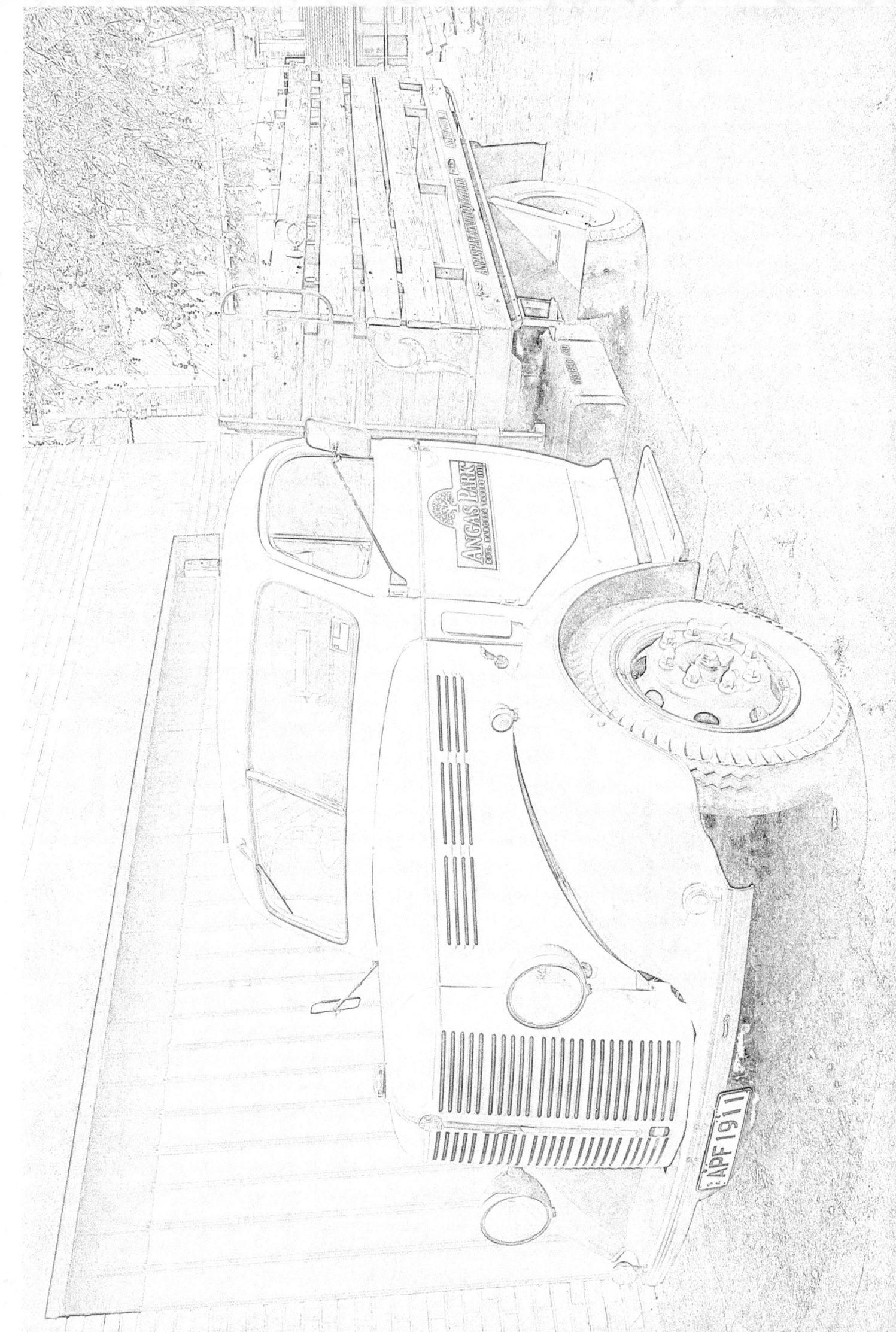

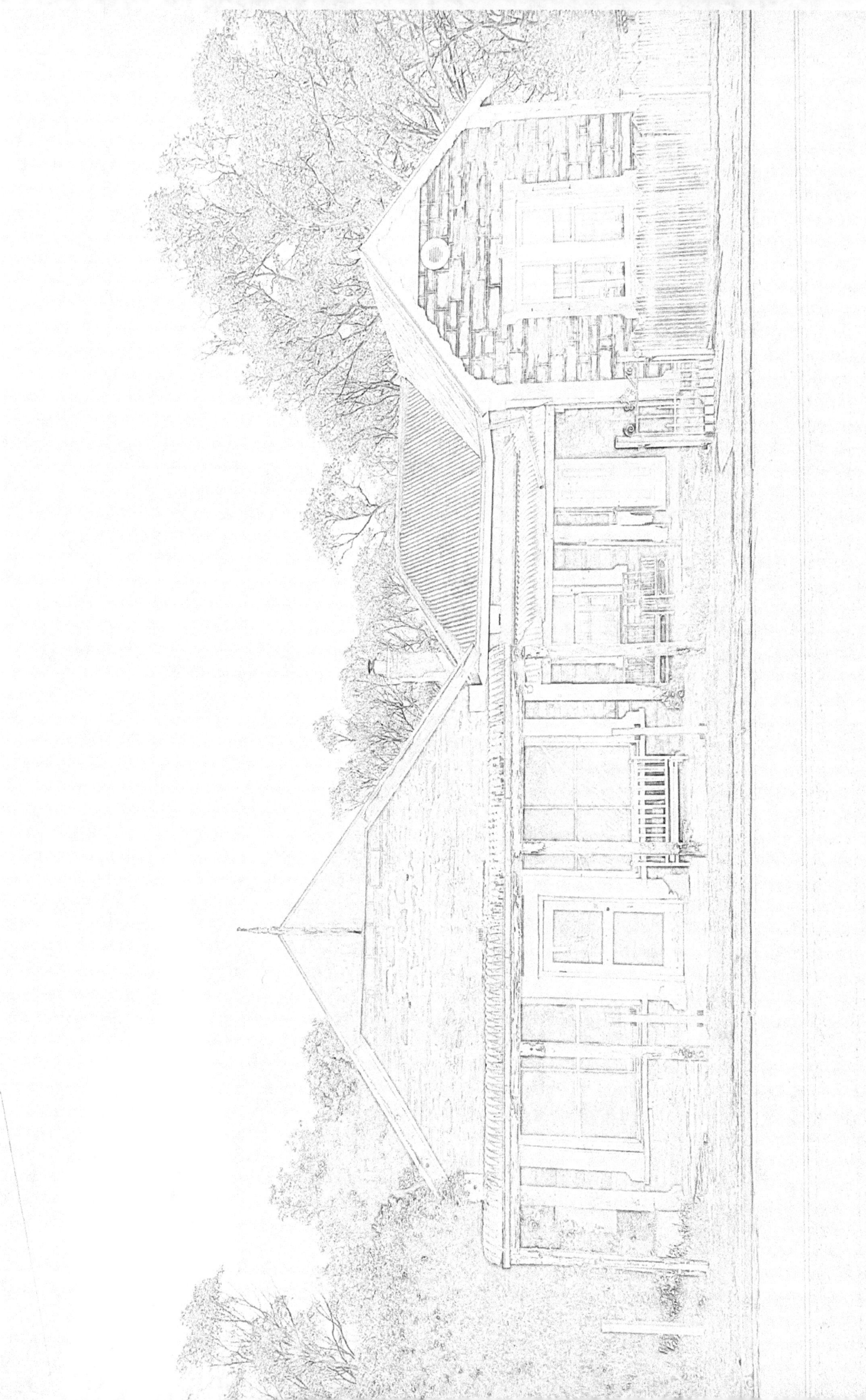

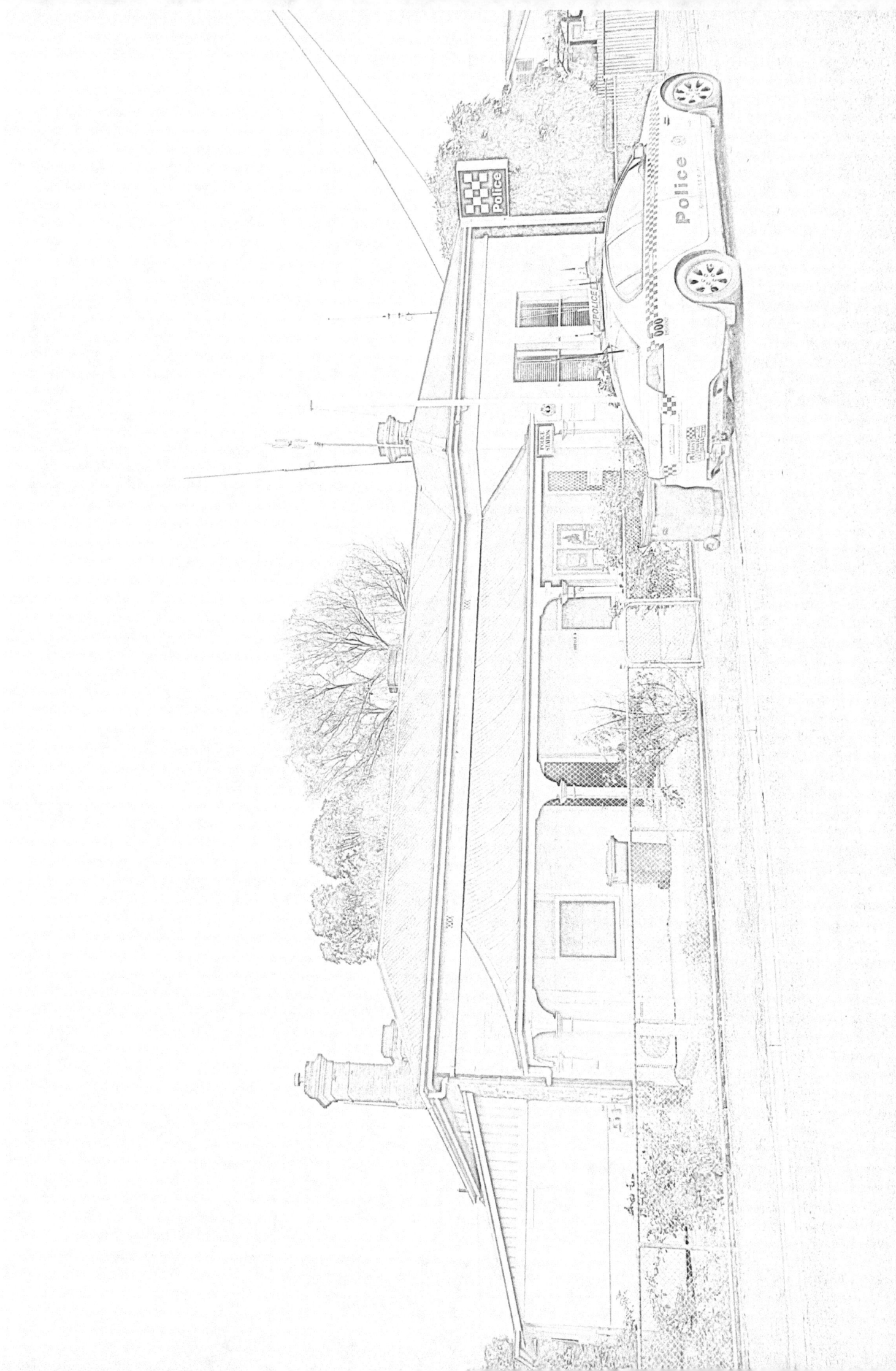

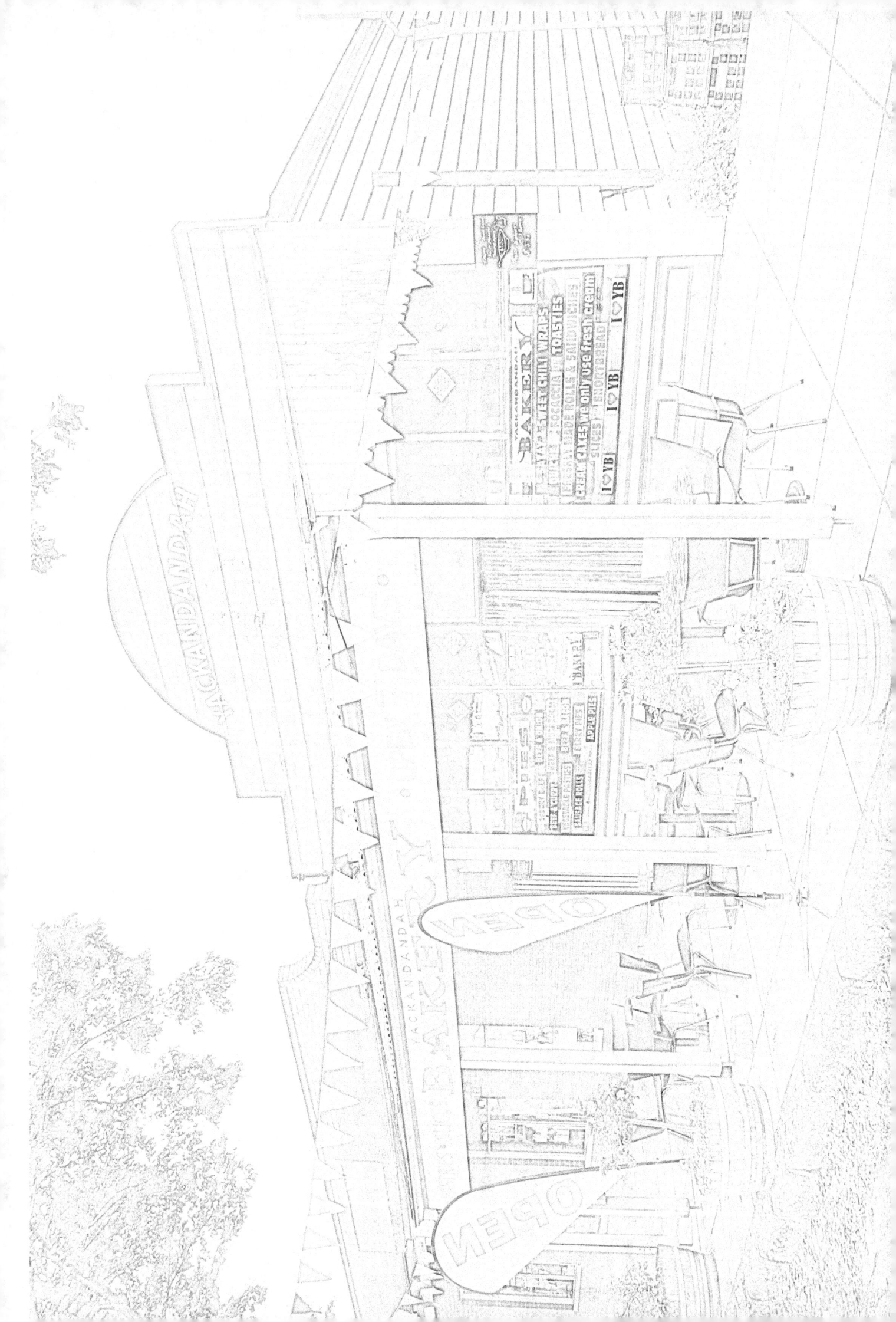

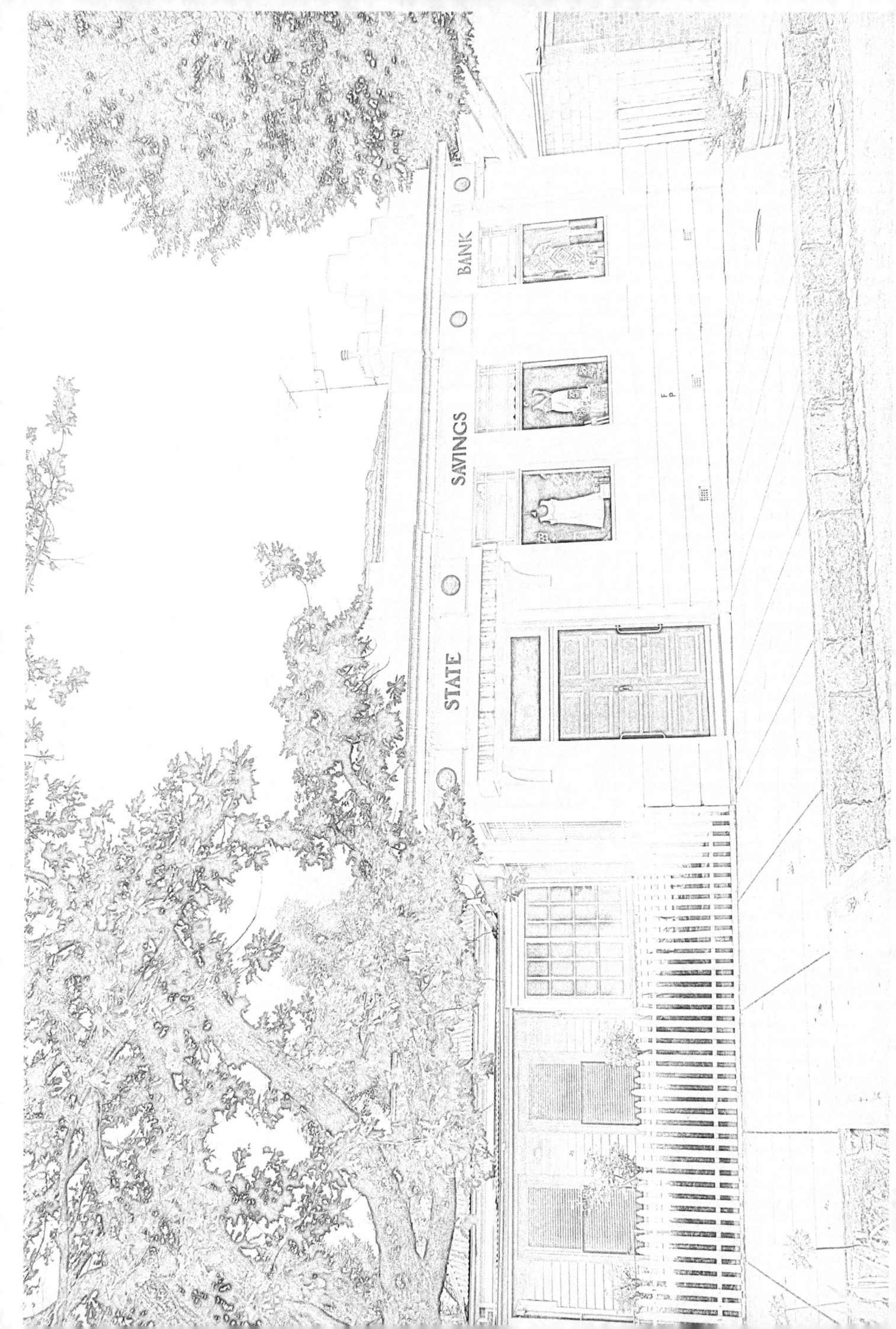

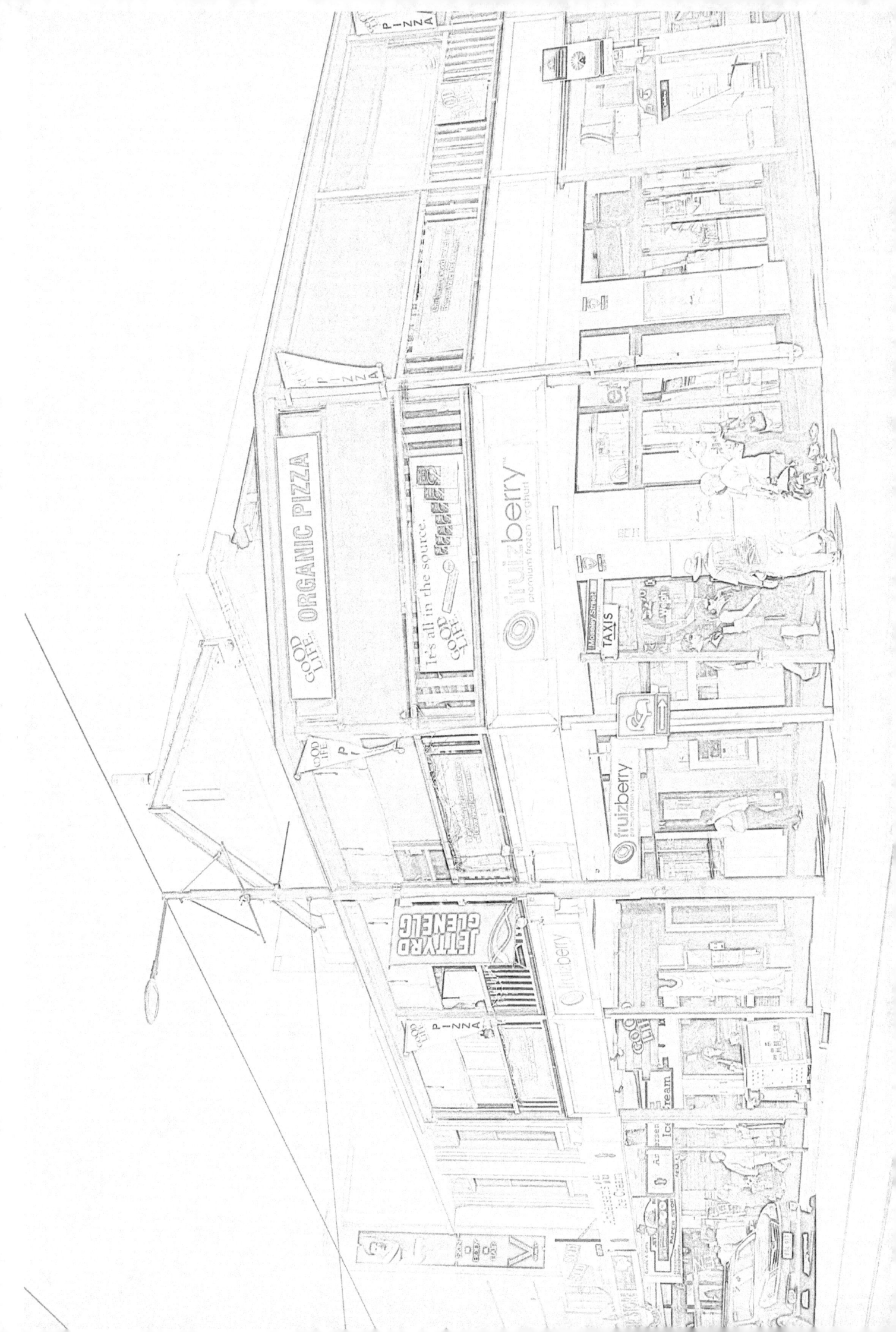

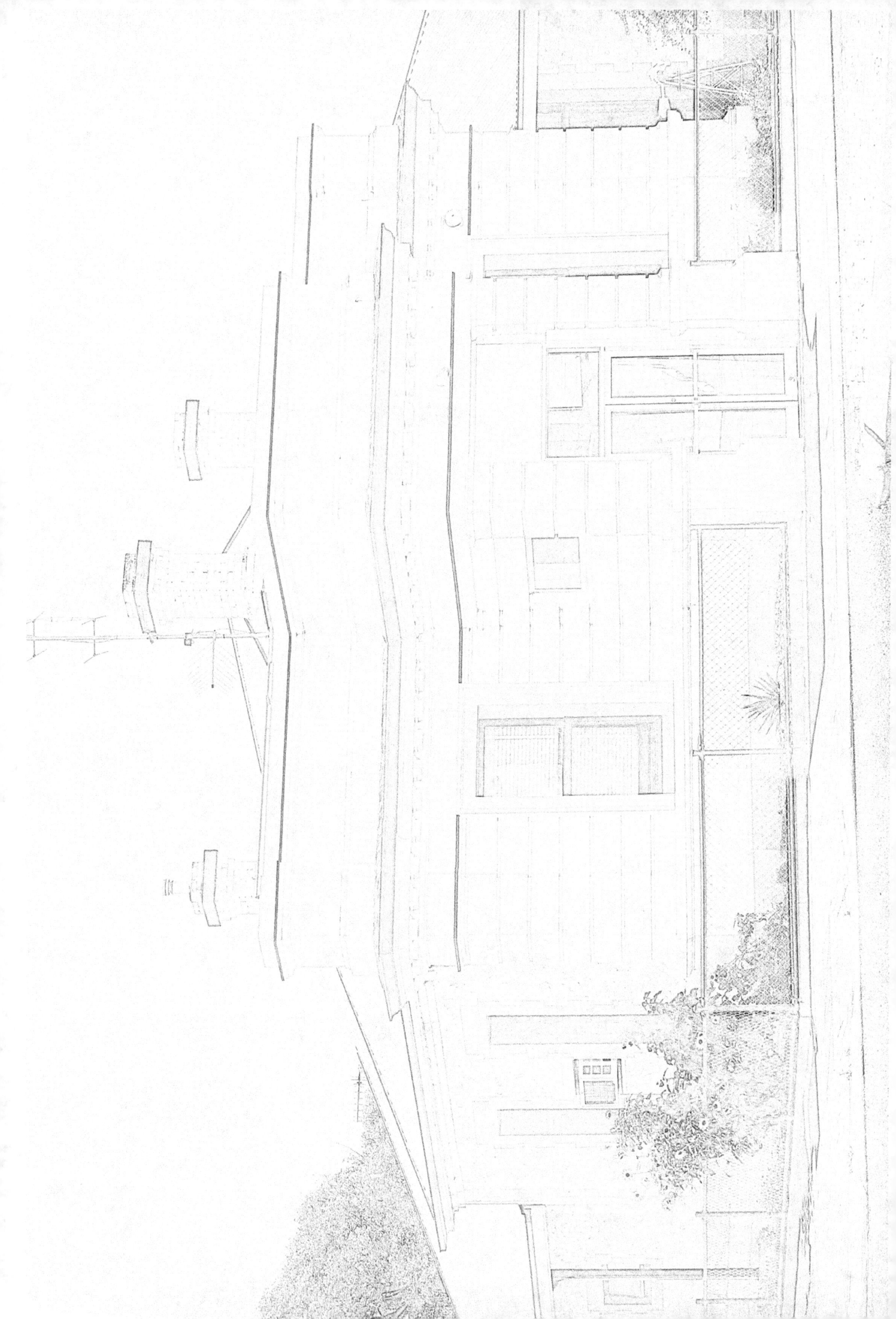